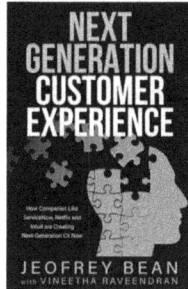

"From the stories of industry pioneers to actionable insights, this book is a treasure trove for anyone aspiring to elevate their customer experience game."
— **Bjorn Granberg, Co-Founder and Co-CEO SkimSafe/SkimSure**

"Jeof has done it again! Whether you are building on the customer experience success you have already or are at the very beginning of this journey, you will find a path with 'Next Generation Customer Experience'. From 'The Customer Experience Revolution' through 'Customer Experience Rules!' to 'Next Generation Customer Experience', Jeof continues his sage insights and 'Bean-isms' that we all love."
— **Sean Van Tyne, Customer Experience Officer at Sitekick; Author of "Easy to Use 2.0," co-author of "The Customer Experience Revolution"**

"Jeof Bean and Vineetha Raveendran's 'Next Generation Customer Experience' is a wonderfully accessible reference to a rich collection of powerful concepts, supporting templates and associated success stories for anyone interested in improving their branded customer experience. This includes valuable insight into the expectations of today's Gen Z consumer and the dramatic impact their expectations have on customer engagement efforts. If you're involved in improving customer experience in any way, you'll find yourself reaching for this book time and time again!"
— **Daniel Shea, Vice-President / Sales & Marketing – International Manufacturing Services, Inc.**

"Like it or not, Gen Z customers are comparing their experience with your company against every other experience they have—via every channel. They expect consistency and they expect you will be able to anticipate their needs. Needs they don't even know they need yet! It's a big ask.

"Jeof packs a punch and shares with you everything you need to know in 'Next Generation Customer Experience'. It's an engaging read with the right mix of research, charts, and stories to bring the learnings to life. You'll dive deep into the emotions, thoughts, beliefs, and feelings of Gen Z customers and how to create customer advocates for your brand. You'll learn the best way to do this is to listen and converse with your customers—in a meaningful way about the things that matter to them.

"If you are looking for ways to make changes in your organization to improve your CX, this will be a resource you will turn to again and again. Like an expert travel guide, 'Next Generation Customer Experience' has many gold nuggets and inspiration on what actions you can take to get the most out of what you are trying to achieve. You'll find the answers here.

"If you are a Customer Experience professional who wants to deepen your knowledge of the changing landscape of customer expectations for Gen Z, everything you need to know is in this book."
   — **Kate Gorman, CX Director, Customer Service Benchmarking Australia (CSBA)**

"'Next Generation Customer Experience' is a must-read for customer experience professionals and businesses aiming to adapt to the expectations of future customers. It covers essential topics such as brand loyalty, the impact of various factors on purchasing decisions, and the role of social media. It also addresses concerns about data privacy and offers valuable insights into the balance between affordability and exceptional customer experiences. This book is a valuable resource for those adapting to the evolving customer landscape and future-focused businesses."
   — **Vivien Francis, Customer Success Manager, ServiceNow**

"I love this book! If you want to grow your business, create meaningful customer experiences for Gen Z, and develop a cadre of customer advocates, Jeof Bean's newest book, 'Next Generation Customer Experience', with Vineetha Raveendran, is exactly what you need.

"The book is insightful and practical and walks you through the 'how-tos' of connecting with Gen Z consumers as a collective generation and as individuals. There are templates outlining key elements of a Customer Experience buyer persona intelligence profile. You and your staff will find these templates are an essential part of the recipe for creating your own branded Customer Experience. Chapter 5 is a curated set of best practices that you can adapt for your business and each chapter is rich with links to meaningful resources to help you put your plans into action. Bean is a gifted author, and the book is both easy to read and inspiring. Do you and your business a huge favor and invest in this book now!"
— **Joely Gardner, Ph.D., CEO and Chief User Experience Researcher of Human Factors Research**

"Jeof Bean and Vineetha Raveendran's 'Next Generation Customer Experience' is timely and breathtakingly original. While practical and grounded, the authors provide an accessible playbook for winning CX strategies in a disruptive reality that is the new normal. If you're seeking transformational impact through CX, you'll find this book indispensable."
— **Samir Asaf, PhD, CFA, CMA, Senior Partner, Regent Financial. Instructor, Corporate Finance, Stanford University**

"Jeof does it again! This book builds on existing CX approaches while introducing the latest concepts and frameworks for CX innovation. A definite must read for all CX professionals and everyone interested in increasing growth, customer advocacy, and profitability!"
— **Dann Allen, Executive CX Strategic Advisor and former CX Executive at MUFG Union Bank and Bank of the West**

NEXT GENERATION
CUSTOMER EXPERIENCE

NEXT
GENERATION
CUSTOMER
EXPERIENCE

How companies like ServiceNow, Netflix and Intuit
are creating next-generation CX now

JEOFREY BEAN

with Vineetha Raveendran

Next Generation Customer Experience:
How Companies Like ServiceNow, Netflix and Intuit are Creating Next-Generation CX Now

© 2024 Jeofrey Bean. All rights reserved.
Published by Del Mar Research, San Diego, CA

ISBN 979-8-9894387-0-9 (paperback)
ISBN 979-8-9894387-1-6 (eBook)
Library of Congress Control Number: 2023924654

DelMarResearch.com

Title: Next generation customer experience : how companies like ServiceNow, Netflix and Intuit are creating next-generation CX now / Jeofrey Bean, with Vineetha Raveendran.

Description: San Diego, CA : Del Mar Research, [2024] | Includes bibliographical references and index.

Identifiers: ISBN: 979-8-9894387-0-9 (paperback) | 979-8-9894387-1-6 (ebook) | LCCN: 2023924654

Subjects: LCSH: Consumer behavior. | Customer services. | Customer relations. | Business enterprises-- Technological innovations. | Consumer satisfaction. | Generation Z. | Success in business. | BISAC: BUSINESS & ECONOMICS / Consumer Behavior. | BUSINESS & ECONOMICS / Customer Relations. | BUSINESS & ECONOMICS / Marketing / Research.

Classification: LCC: HF5415.32 .B43 2024 | DDC: 658.8342--dc23

Publication managed by AuthorImprints.com

In Memory of Larry Tesler
1945-2020

A computer scientist who focused on human–computer interaction. His groundbreaking work helped create modern customer and user experiences with technology and always with people in mind. His body of work is enormous. It includes the invention of the cut-and-paste computer function, the first word processor with a graphical user interface and Tesler's law, otherwise known as the law of conservation of complexity. Tesler stated that "for any system there is a certain amount of complexity which cannot be reduced."

He worked at Xerox PARC and then joined Apple Computer working with Steve Jobs. After that he was hired by Amazon and worked with Jeff Bezos as vice president of shopping experience. If you previewed a book on Amazon, you have experienced one of Tesler's original works.

After being with a couple more businesses, he became an independent consultant helping Silicon Valley companies design and develop user experiences. That was what he was doing when I (Jeof) had the pleasure of interviewing him with my coauthor for the "Customer Experience Revolution" book. He was kind and tremendously insightful. He appreciated our questions. The interview was scheduled for 45 minutes. It was an amazing two-hour conversation about customer and user experience that remains a powerful inspiration.

If you use a computer or phone, on the Internet and off, you have benefitted from Larry's work. Most likely every day. He created the foundation for exemplary customer and user experiences for generations of devices, software and people to come. We are incredibly fortunate.

Table of Contents

List of Figures

Foreword

J eofrey Bean is a pioneer of contemporary Customer Experience. *The Customer Experience Revolution* was one of the first books on the subject and is still used in boardrooms and classrooms today around the world as a standard for customer experience leadership. It was my honor and pleasure to work with Jeof on this. We were fortunate to meet some extraordinary people along the way who shared their stories about customer experience achievements that became the insights of how their companies have changed business forever. I have many fond and wonderful memories of our collaboration.

Well, Jeof has done it again! Whether you are building on the customer experience success you have already or are at the very beginning of this journey, you will find a path with *Next Generation Customer Experience*. From *The Customer Experience Revolution* through *Customer Experience Rules!*, Jeof continues his sage insights and "Bean-isms" that we all love.

To be clear, this is *not* an academic book. It is a practical and innovative publication based on Jeof's many years of experience in advanced marketing and customer experience development combined with interviews with leading customer experience professionals creating next-generation customer experiences now.

With *Next Generation Customer Experience (NGCX)*, Jeof answers the question, "What is essential to create an engaging and profitable next-generation customer experience?" He gracefully guides us through concepts like The Customer Experience Effect—the impact of desirable experiences on increasing advocacy, helping to expand business revenues while reducing the costs of marketing, sales, new customer acquisition and support. NGCX hits that sweet spot of customer desirability, business viability and technological feasibility.

One of the inspirations for this book was Jeof's interest in Gen Z, also called iGen, the internet generation. This generation began about 1995 and is more different than any other generations compared. Jeof, along with colleague and contributing author, Vineetha Raveendran, conducted interviews and research to develop a better understanding of this generation. Their conclusions will help businesses develop engaging next generation customer experiences.

As long as I have known Jeof, one of his mantras has been "the secret to differentiating your brand is by offering experiences that are not easily replicated on and off the internet." In *Next Generation Customer Experience*, he explains how critical capabilities of creating effective and sustainable next-generation customer experiences are developing and using customer experience intelligence (CXI). CXI is a cultural and systematic combination of internal and external inputs from customers, about all the interactions they have with your business, on the internet and off. CXI is based in turning near-real-time or real-time customer data—including "thick data," internal data and big data that provide insights to improve and innovate customer experiences.

As Jeof has been telling us for years, he reaffirms with *Next Generation Customer Experience* to go deep into a "contextual" understanding of your customers and explains how that leads to integrating your company's people, products and services into their life and their business. He identifies and explains the "say-do gap"—the gap between what people say they will do and what they actually do. He recommends understanding differences that may be in the customer say-do gap. He recommends using at least four dimensions to improve the understanding of customer interactions with the "CX4." The "CX4" includes the value of the customer interaction, the range of emotions people experience while having the interaction, the customer perception of how the interaction used their time, and the "Do-For/Do-To"—what the customer believes an interaction did for or to them.

There are many types of input methods for understanding and developing the experiences of our customers, guests and patients. Jeof explains that whichever set of inputs we choose, they need to fit into our company culture, budget, and mesh with other available resources. *Next Generation Customer Experience* shows us how to "measure what matters to our customers." Gaining insight from the latest thought leaders in behavioral economics and more, Jeof shows us how human experience comes *before* the economic outcome. Testing how people will react to your economic offer and the interactions related to it, *before* you scale-up your decisions, can reduce guesswork and minimize risk for you and the customer.

We live in an interesting time of "information at our fingertips." Streaming across all platforms, both digital and analog, we are constantly bombarded with information. In *Next Generation Customer Experience* it is explained that "the person who controls the options that are presented to us controls our behavior and our decisions. We may think that we have free will but contextual cues in the design are responsible for a big part of our behavior." Here there is practical guidance for us to build online decision-making choices that are desirable, rewarding and ethical—test the choices and default settings while they are being developed.

Jeof reminds us that the late, great, Steve Jobs shared that "You've got to start with the customer experience and work backward to the technology. You can't start with the technology then try to figure out where to sell it." In the end, next generation Experience Makers (think Ally Bank, Apple, Intuit, Netflix and ServiceNow) 'combined insights from behavior, technology and economics for developing experiences for people.' As individuals and organizations, we need to be relevant and valuable now and into the future. There are insightful people, paths, and resources to help you get there. God bless Steve Jobs, Jeofrey Bean, and the *Next Generation Customer Experience.*

—Sean Van Tyne

Sean Van Tyne is the Customer Experience Officer at SiteKick and the author of *Easy to Use 2.0*, co-author of *The Customer Experience Revolution: How Companies Like Apple, Amazon, and Starbucks Have Changed Business Forever*, and a contributing author to *The Guide to the Product Management and Marketing Body of Knowledge.*

Introduction

Next-generation customers are unlike all those before them. From the early to mid-1990s, when the people of this generation were born, the internet was already in wide use around the world. Known as Generation Z, or Gen Z, and sometimes iGens, they've become the largest generation, constituting 32 percent of the global population—or 2.47 billion of the 7.7 billion people on Earth—surpassing the Millennials and Baby Boomers, respectively.[1]

This generation is keenly aware of the differences between acceptable and unacceptable customer experiences (or, as we will refer to them throughout the book, CX), whether on the internet or off. From their viewpoints and based on their behavior as customers, there is no middle ground between companies known as experience makers—those who clearly strive to set new standards for making customers happy and enhancing their lives—and companies who are focused on business as usual.

Gen Z consumers have distinct and important characteristics that may surprise you. If you want to develop engaging and profitable experiences for them, their characteristics need to be looked at as a collective generation and as individuals, whether your organization wants to engage and serve customers, users, clients, guests or patients. Failure to understand the people of Gen Z risks being separated from them or never connecting with them.

Our experience as CX practitioners and educators and our interviews with people at companies leading the way in customer experience led us to a question we were inspired to answer with this book: What else complements technology and the people of Gen Z and is essential to creating an engaging and profitable next-generation customer experience?

We found that there are next generation capabilities that are being used now by many customer experience leaders, early-stage companies and ourselves to develop successful next-generation experiences. These capabilities are not implemented alone. Customer experience leaders use a specially selected combination of these complementary aspects to create future customer experiences. They do it with an understanding of the most successful leaders, who have architected futures by designing or guiding creation of new products, services, technologies, systems and experiences that people adopt as the new way of getting things done, living their lives or doing business. That recognition is that "the future is not fact; it is a decision."[2] And from our perspective, that decision is to apply many of the advanced capabilities in the development of next-generation customer experiences.

One of those capabilities is The Customer Experience Effect. This is the awareness and ability to benefit from the potential value customer experience can contribute. It includes the impact of desirable customer and user experiences on increasing customer advocacy, helping to expand business revenues while reducing the costs of marketing, sales, new customer acquisition and support. Additionally, companies benefit by differentiating themselves by offering customer experiences that are not easily replicated.

Another critical capability of creating successful and sustainable next-generation customer experiences is developing and using customer experience intelligence or CXI. It's a cultural and systematic combination of internal and external inputs from customers, about all of the interactions they have with your business, on the internet and off. It is based on near-real-time or real-time capturing of customer feedback and other selected data. A portfolio approach of selected complementary information inputs including thick data, internal data and big data, with insights developed from the data sources, can improve existing customer experiences and innovate interactions and strategies.

Additionally, we find that many leading customer experience and user experience organizations, small and large, use a new type of economics, behavioral economics. With its hallmark combination of human (customer) behavior and economics, the advantage this gives is already recognized by some CX leaders including Intuit, Tesla and ServiceNow. Behavioral economics is used in place of or in addition to conventional economics and offers the potential to have more success with customer experience and a valuable competitive advantage. Richard Thaler—professor of behavioral science and economics at the University of Chicago and winner of the Nobel Prize for Economics—developed this new and more effective theory of economics, along with several other people. Yet it was Thaler who proved to many people, including other economists and astute businesspeople, the importance of including human behavior to make more accurate, prescriptive and predictive economic decisions. Understanding and using behavioral economics to develop and sustain extraordinary customer experiences is at an early stage. This means advantages and profitable opportunities are plentiful for those who grasp and apply it. Here we provide an introduction to it.

Along with understanding the customer experience effect, having effective customer experience intelligence and applying behavioral economics to decision-making, those focusing on next-generation customer experiences consistently apply and create CX best practices to determine, develop and deliver successful experiences. A best practice is a habit, priority or process that is proven to be very effective in attaining superior results with customer experience.

The results include growing the number of customer advocates, increasing profit margins and lowering the cost of acquiring new customers. Customer experience best practices can be developed inside an organization and learned from others.

A carefully selected set of best practices is included in Chapter 5. This can be the foundation of best practices you choose to use or in addition to what is already working well for you now. Start with one or select several. Integrate them into your organization's decision-making processes of determining, developing or improving customer experiences.

Another critical capability for effective next-generation organizations is developing strategies and tactics for positive customer interconnections. There are many ways organizations purposely create positive customer interactions. Their processes for developing them not just once but many times is frequently unique, like a genetic code.

Our discussion of this is about a specific, proven process that is customer-focused throughout. It applies to all the parts of the customer experience continuum to develop: messages, people, processes, technologies, products and services. This approach to strategies and interconnection is improved when partnered with the customer experience intelligence portfolio discussed earlier.

Lastly, in Chapter 7, is innovation. This chapter sets out to answer the questions: How does successful customer experience innovation happen? What are some examples of companies that are leading customer experience innovators?

Think about companies like ServiceNow, Pedego, Square, Course-Key, Uber or Intuit. Is there a characteristic that these successful customer experience innovators share that is obtainable by others? And what is the difference between old-school and next-generation customer experience innovation?

The concept of being disruptive with innovation is popular but frequently misunderstood. Customer experience innovators keep a very clear understanding of what it means to be an effective disruptor. The important detailed explanation for this is included.

Being a next-generation customer experience leader is a decision and a commitment to start right here and now—to be profitable and to enhance people's lives with customer experiences.

Apple Inc.'s founders Steve Jobs and Steve Wozniak committed to creating a customer experience revolution in computers and phones by adapting technology to customers. The intuitive design of Apple products barely requires any instruction to be able to use. This was in stark contrast to early PCs and phones that were obtuse and often counterintuitive. This changed people's personal and working lives for the better.

Intuit changed the lives of businesspeople doing accounting, taxes and tax filing with its Quicken and TurboTax software platforms. Intuit was started by Scott Cook and Tom Proulx. Like the people at Apple, they had the belief that software should be so intuitively obvious that people know how to use it with minimal to no instruction.

Then there is Square, the company that opened the market for mobile payments. Jack Dorsey began the company with the idea that using mobile software and devices to give and take payments should be easy for everyone involved.

More recent examples include Pedego and SkimSure. Don DiCostanzo had the idea that purchasing, keeping and using an electric bicycle should be a pleasurable experience. He founded the Pedego electric bicycle company. Purposely serving a rapidly expanding active senior population, Pedego is likely the first in the e-bike industry to have dedicated dealerships.

Bjorn Granberg and Carl Martinson had experiences that led them to start SkimSafe in Europe and SkimSure in the United States to make it simple for people to protect their credit card and other dig- itized data from data-skimming thieves at home or while traveling. This protection is conveniently enabled by carrying a card that looks just like a regular credit or debit card. The card jams the signals of skimming devices used by thieves trying to collect information off credit cards and other data sources people carry.

> **There are many practical and innovative insights to learn from these customer experience leaders and their companies. Those insights can be bolstered with an understanding of wider views of effective leadership.**

There are many practical and innovative insights to learn from these customer experience leaders and their companies. Those in- sights can be bolstered with an understanding of wider views of effective leadership, like those from Pulitzer Prize-winning biogra- pher, historian and journalist Doris Kearns Goodwin. Goodwin has researched and written insightful biographies of leaders for over 50 years: "Leadership is the ability to use talent, skills and emotional intelligence to mobilize people to a common purpose. And hope- fully, if you are the kind of leader that we want people to be, that common purpose is to make a positive difference in people's lives."[3]

This book is meant to help you navigate to a leadership position with next-generation customer experience. Whether you are build- ing on the customer experience success you have now or are at the very beginning of your process, a good place to start is inside the following chapters. Enjoy!

Next Generation Customer Experience
Reader Journey

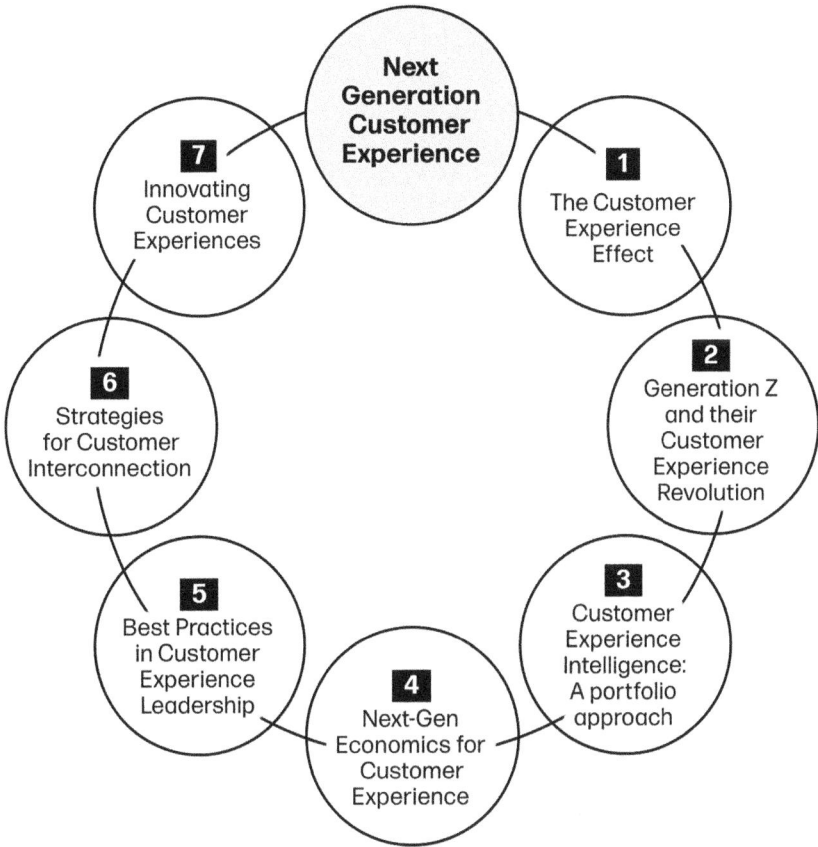

Reader journey recommendations. While each chapter can be read individually, and in any order you choose, it is recommended that the chapters be read in the order presented above to get the most from your reader journey. Read chapter 3, Customer Experience Intelligence, before reading chapter 6, Strategies for Customer Interconnection, to get the most context and insights from each.

The Customer Experience Effect

Being better, different and more valuable through customer experience

"The number one driver of our growth at Zappos has been repeat customers and word of mouth. Our philosophy has been to take most of the money we would have spent on paid advertising and invest it into customer service and the customer experience instead, letting our customers do the marketing for us through word of mouth."

— Tony Hsieh, internet entrepreneur and venture capitalist, retired as CEO of Zappos in August 2020 after 21 years

CHAPTER 1 Overview

What is customer experience? Defined by experience makers	Extraordinary customer experiences increase measurable brand value	Views of customer experience return on investment	Learn from leaders and start-ups Amazon, Netflix, ServiceNow, SkimSure	Transform to customer experience along a continuum

Online shoe and clothing company Zappos's revenues and profit margins are higher than the competition since their active customer advocacy rates are typically in double digits. This drives down the firm's cost of marketing, sales and acquiring new customers. Zappos belongs to a unique group of businesses that are customer experience makers. The customers of these companies, whether consumers or businesses, online or offline, stay customers for a significantly longer time, usually adopting the firms as part of how they live their lives or run their businesses. Their strong interconnection with customers boosts their corporate valuations and builds brand equity.

Many experience makers began that way as start-ups: think REI, Amazon, Netflix, Apple and Workday. Others focus on their expertise—such as product innovation, customer service, technology or price—and then transform into experience makers in the way of Ally Bank, ServiceNow and Microsoft's business productivity systems. While these examples are more well-known, many lesser-known businesses, small and large, have made the change to competing with a difficult-to-duplicate customer experience. Their goal is to become better and different for customers and more profitable and longer-lasting than their competitors.

What is customer experience?

The authors' definition of customer experience is developed based on a careful look at the aggregate view of the companies that are most successful at delivering a memorable customer experience and on interviews with people at many of these firms including their customers.

The process began in 2011 while writing the book "The Customer Experience Revolution," for which the research and interviews with people at leading customer experience companies made it obvious that existing customer experience definitions were not adequate.

Since then, while working with clients to fix, improve and innovate customer experiences and directing over 160 projects worldwide with the same objectives as part of a course on customer experience at the University of California San Diego Division of Extended Studies, our definition has been continuously updated to more accurately reflect its relationship to customer loyalty and advocacy.

As defined by leading customer experience makers, customer experience (CX) is:

The feelings, thoughts, beliefs and memories people have about all their interactions with or about a company's messages, people, processes, products or services.

When does the experience start? From the time a person discovers the company to when they become a customer and onward to becoming an advocate for the company.

The user experience (UX) is included in the customer experience. There are typically two kinds: a person's experience directly interacting with a company's products or services; and interacting with an organization's web site, mobile app, digital kiosk or other devices.

Customer Experience (CX) Defined by the Experience Makers
The feelings, thoughts, beliefs and memories people have about all their interactions **with** or **about** a company's messages, people, processes and technologies, products or services. (The customer experience continuum is an organization's people, processes and technologies, products or services)

When does the experience start?
- From the time a person discovers the company.
- Then when they become a customer and on to being an advocate.

The User Experience (UX) is included in the customer experience. There are usually two kinds:
- A person's experience directly interacting with a company's products or services
- Interacting with an organization's web site, mobile app, digital kiosk or other devices.

FIGURE 1.1 Customer experience defined by experience makers

The definition of customer experience has four essential pieces.

1) The components of customer experience. These include the feelings, thoughts, beliefs and memories people have about all their interactions with or about a company's messages, people, processes/technologies, products or services. Messages, people, processes/technologies and products or services make up the customer experience continuum, which we will explore later. The "with" and "about" parts of the definition are extremely important as people can interact directly with the company or have experiences indirectly with it through other people, professional reviews, social media and many other ways.

2) The customer experience starts before a person is a customer. We estimate that 80% to 85% of businesses and organizations believe that the experience begins when a purchase of a product or service is made. But customer experience makers think quite differently. They realize that people have experiences with and about a company before becoming a customer—experiences that are factors in determining whether they actually become one.

3) The fostering of advocacy. A person's end-to-end or ongoing relationship with a business has been called their customer journey. This journey begins when they first discover a company and continues through all interactions with or about the business to when, hopefully, they become an energized advocate for the company.

4) User experience is a critical piece of CX. Before and within the customer experience are very important user experiences. The user experience can be one of using a company's products or services but it can also involve interactions with a company's website or mobile app. The user experience provides the proof that the promises made during the customer experience have been delivered.

CX pioneer: Picoult—one of the first to show the value of investing in CX

In response to many businesses pretending to care about customer experiences by paying mere lip service to the concept of it, and others serious about investing in it and wanting to understand the value of CX, Jon Picoult, founder of Watermark Consulting and a customer experience valuation pioneer, built an index that showed the value and advantages to businesses that invested in and competed with a great customer experience.

Picoult's index arose from his firm's Customer Experience ROI Study, which was created to get executives to focus not only on the cost/benefit of specific customer experience initiatives but to reach what Picoult describes as "the macro impact of an effective customer experience strategy." The index compares the cumulative total stock returns for two model portfolios—the top 10 (Leaders) and bottom 10 (Laggards) of publicly traded companies in customer experience. The Leaders and Laggards were selected using Forrester Research's Customer Experience Index beginning in 2007, later adding the Temkin Group's Customer Experience Ratings and Qualtrics XMI data in 2016 and 2019, respectively. Each of these CX rankings is based on surveys of 10,000 or more U.S. consumers. The 2021 Customer Experience ROI Study represents over 12 years of customer experience data. Here are some of the insights.

- CX Leaders outperformed the broader stock market, generating a total return 108 points higher than the S&P 500. CX Laggards trailed far behind, posting a total return 110 points lower than the broader market. CX Leaders generated a total cumulative return 3.4 times greater than that of the CX Laggards.
- CX Leaders gain increased revenue because happy and loyal customers stay with them, are less price-sensitive and want more products and services from them. A high percentage of these customers are active advocates, which results in

increased revenue and decreased cost of sales and marketing to acquire new customers.

- CX Laggards struggle to raise revenue, have low retention, high price sensitivity, limited cross-purchasing, negative advocacy and higher costs to acquire new customers and deal with unhappy ones.[4]

> **Brand equity refers to a premium value that a company generates for products or services based on their recognizable name[5] and customer experiences associated with it.**

Extraordinary customer experiences increase measurable brand value

People experience your brand before they are customers, while they are customers and when and if they become your brand ambassadors. How they experience your brand in these three stages will impact its measurable value. If you are not interested in brand value or building it as an asset, then think of your company's reputation and what it means for sales, customer advocacy and reducing the cost of acquiring new customers.

Brand consultancy Interbrand tracks and publishes rankings of brand equity in its annual Best Global Brands index. In 2021, five of the 10 largest risers in brand value ranking were experience-maker companies: Amazon, Spotify, Netflix, Apple and Salesforce. Their respective brand values are: Amazon $M200,667; Spotify $M8,389; Netflix $M12,665; Apple $M322,999; and Salesforce $M10,755.[6]

The global brand growth during the turbulent 2020-2021 period was the largest Interbrand has ever reported since it began tracking brand value. The combined value of the top 100 brands increased 15% from 2020 to 2021. The growth and total value leaders are technology companies and Interbrand emphasized that "the digital trends that have underpinned strong growth in this sector show no sign of abating and the different professional and personal ways in which consumers rely on cloud-based technology, artificial intelligence, streaming and subscription-based services bolster this sector."

Yet most of these companies are not just tech organizations. They are focused on customer and user experience. They set a high bar for delivering an outstanding customer and user experience, even higher than what is expected or delivered by others in their market.

This includes Apple, with an annual brand value growth rate of 26% to $408,250 million; Amazon, whose value was up by 24%, reaching $249,249 million and user experience leader Google, up 19% at $196,811 million. The faster risers for increasing brand value have CX leaders Tesla, Salesforce, Amazon and Apple. Interbrand points to Tesla as an example of a firm that demonstrates "how successful brands woo consumers with a clear, coherent vision. Even with anecdotal reports of reliability issues, Tesla customers score high satisfaction, significantly above peers in this sector."[7]

Interbrand describes valuable brand differentiation as "distinctiveness, the existence of uniquely ownable signature assets and experiences that are recognized and remembered by customers and difficult to replicate."

Customer empathy is a characteristic common to the distinctiveness of experience makers and brand value-building. Interbrand argues that "customer empathy has never been a more critical component of brand-building." They stress that it takes companies with a keen understanding of customers to anticipate the almost constant changes in priorities and emotions and then confidently improve or innovate interactions or strategies. The insights from customer experience intelligence (CXI) deliver an understanding of customers that helps a company make effective improvements or innovations in interactions and strategies, increasing customer connection and brand valuations.

And, looking at the new entrants and companies that have reentered Interbrand's index of brand value, it's clear that experience-maker companies are having a big impact. YouTube, Tesla and Instagram are notable for their achievements in elevating the experiences they deliver to customers. These brands have created and grown a successful interconnection with specific types of customers.

Customer experience leadership transcends market currency and what customers expect

Where customer experience makers create new industries or enter existing markets, the currency consumers and business customers care most about, along with money, changes from a product, service or pricing focus to expectations of customer experience. These expectations do not necessarily have to come from a customer experience leader inside the same industry or market. Consumers and business customers learn and raise their expectations as customers, patients and guests from the exceptionally good experiences they have with all companies, regardless of industry or market. If you are a customer experience leader in one market or industry, chances are you are setting experience expectations for many others in which you're not even operating. This is partly because people typically do not restrict their comparisons of experiences by industry or categorize them into separate buckets such as business-to-business, business-to-consumer or a specific market.

Views of customer experience return on investment (ROI)

There are many views on CX ROI and how to measure it. Searching the internet or attending trade shows or conferences for advice and original thinking on the subject reveals a special set of companies and people, innovators in customer experience, who have given CX ROI some careful thought and have applied their expert approaches to it. Here is a sampling of some of their insights.

Delivering desirable experiences lets companies command up to a 16% price premium on their products and services, according to professional services firm PricewaterhouseCoopers (PwC) in their report The Future of Customer Experience. This premium does not include the benefits from increased loyalty and reductions in costs from customer support and in new customer acquisition. "In the U.S., even when people love a company or product, 59% will walk away after several bad experiences, 17% after just one bad experience. 32% of all customers would stop doing business with a brand they loved after one bad experience." This highlights the risk of not providing experiences that meet or exceed customer expectations, including those set by customer experience leaders in other industries. These disappointing encounters can create un-advocacy, where unfavorable word of mouth or reviews on or off the internet produce a negative return on investment.[8]

It's likely that independent research firm Forrester created the first customer experience index (its CX Index™). And recently, when evaluating the experiences customers were having, Forrester found that they are 2.4 times more likely to stay with companies that solve their problems more quickly than competitors. And 2.7 times more likely to spend more when businesses show that they understand them and communicate to them clearly. Forrester also found that "when employees in physical locations answer all customer questions" customers are 10 times more likely to recommend that organization.[9] This increase in customer advocacy is a central goal of investing in and delivering a pleasing customer experience. The advocacy increases a company's growth while lowering the costs associated with new customer acquisition.

Another dimension to consider about customer experience return on investment is your overall cost to serve customers. Consulting firm Deloitte found that "offering a high-quality customer experience can lower the cost of serving customers by up to 33%."

Cost-to-serve, associated with customer experiences, can be increased or decreased. The costs of interactions can be evaluated and the interactions changed or modified depending on what an organization's customer experience intelligence and cost factors indicate.[10]

And then there is the ROI specific to being customer experience-centric online. Deloitte finds that customer experience is the most important factor in a business's digital transformation success and a likely predictor of success "since client-centric companies are 60% more profitable compared to companies not focused on the customer."[11]

Finding your CX return on investment (ROI)

It takes commitment and objectivity to get an indication of what a specific CX return on investment could be for your organization. Start by looking at a part of the business and its related metrics and the metrics that customers care about (more about this later in the book). Select the metrics that are impacted by customer interactions. Next, select a flow of customer experience intelligence related to those metrics and customer experience interactions. This includes baselining the present experience from the customer's viewpoint. You will use the insights, numbers and words from the CXI to create recommendations for improving the interactions based on customer interaction goals. The goals you set are desired outcomes for you and the customer that are linked to the set of metrics that are impacted by the customer interactions you selected earlier. After making the improvements to the interactions you will need some time to see their impact. How much time will depend on several factors including the business you are in, the market(s) and customers you serve and how much proof your organization decides it needs for an objective conclusion. (For more information about this see Chapter 3 and Chapter 6.)

Learn from the leaders

Whether you aspire to be a large-scale customer experience leader or are looking to earn sustainable value and hard-to-copy differentiation for customers in a more modest realm, there is plenty to learn from the large CX leaders like Amazon and Netflix. Both began as start-up ideas by selling books and renting DVDs online, respectively. Each has sustained their customer experience leadership by evolving and transforming their interactions with new and existing customers. Whether through innovating new experiences or improving the relevancy and value of existing ones, continuously refreshing the customer experience life cycle is part of the business. While examples of this could fill many books, here are some that show leadership in CX thinking and its value.

Charlie Ward, an engineer at Amazon, kept puzzling over how to remove the biggest barriers to online shopping. Ward focused on reducing the cost and time of shipping for customers and as a result invented Amazon Prime. What is Prime's big "do-for" for customers? "Amazon Prime takes the effort out of ordering," according to Amazon Founder and CEO Jeff Bezos' early web post about the new service option to pay an annual fee to get free shipping. At the time of this writing, that annual fee is $139 and also includes streaming media services and Prime Day shopping for an estimated 150 million Prime subscribers. Amazon is valued at $1.5 trillion.

After looking carefully at Amazon and the origin and success of Prime, Jason Aten, technology columnist for Inc. magazine, concluded that "Focusing on investing in your customers is such a great way to evaluate the cost of every new initiative. Whenever you invest in elevating the customer experience in a meaningful way, like by reducing friction or frustration, you add value. That value leads to loyalty, which—over time—leads to more business."[12]

Netflix has consistently been a leader in the brutally competitive streaming content market and customer experience has played a major part in growing revenues and retaining a leadership position for over two decades. For example, as large as YouTube is, with 21% of all global video streaming traffic, Netflix has 26%. Since its inception in 1997, Netflix has invested in understanding every customer interaction, resulting in a massive data set that gives the company a unique view and insights to present and future customer experiences.

And today, the people at Netflix work as hard as ever to understand customers so they can innovate experiences for them and keep the company's industry standing. As recognized in an evaluation by financial services firm Morningstar: "Through the streaming video delivery method, Netflix tracks every customer interaction, from large (total time spent at Netflix) to minute (whether a user pressed fast-forward). This data is aggregated in massive cloud databases throughout the world. Netflix can query this information to better understand network and device performance, customer behavior and content popularity."

Netflix has these customer intelligence inputs in near real-time.[13] They can quickly develop insights, make decisions and take actions from strategic to tactical and at the interaction level in near real time too. The company can iterate on this cycle of inputs to actions more quickly than most competitors—a fact that explains its sustained leadership and value creation despite a narrow competitive moat.[14]

The outstanding performance of many of the top customer experience companies has been helpful to the organizations we have worked with, who are committed to customer experience now and for the next generation and have drawn guidance and inspiration from these role-model firms for practical learning, objective-setting and developing measures of success.

What works as a cross-functional CX transformation accelerator?

All companies provide customer experiences—most of them are transactional, performed and delivered by default. But a purposely created customer experience, on the other hand, with interactions developed to please customers and make the business different and better for them, is an extraordinary one. It both causes people to become advocates for the company and lower costs associated with profitably growing the business. ServiceNow has successfully made the transformation to focusing on and benefitting from delivering extraordinary and purposely developed customer experience, doing it in sizable and manageable chunks. The company, a provider of digital IT, employee and customer workflows to businesses, began as a start-up in 2004 and has grown from 5,000 employees in 2016 to over 13,000 in 2020.[15] It has annual revenues of $4.8 billion.[16]

While speaking with the company's Teena Singh, senior manager of customer insights and adoption, about aspects most critical to ServiceNow's successful transformation, she stressed how effective cross-functional, horizontal communications were in garnering support and getting many departments to move in sync. That happened, she says, when people realized that "we have to get together and rethink how we communicate to customers." This was the springboard to get the company into a reevaluation mode.

Some internal changes had customer impacts that needed to be communicated quickly and meaningfully. For instance, Singh says, "How do you announce newly available technology in a customer-centric way? What are the right marketing points? What is the messaging?" Based on the insights from customer experience intelligence, Singh's team found that while there are many important communication channels for reaching external customers, along with sending messages directly to them, messages sent out through specific social media platforms that customers care about, like LinkedIn and Twitter, are very effective for expanding their reach.

Citing another instance where messaging helped accelerate the transformation, Singh recalls how in-app feedback and customer interviews alerted them that customers were really frustrated with how the company told them about specific things. "What really made the transformation get to the next level was taking the problems that we had agreed on—including all the internal departments involved, including product development—and securing executive sponsorship, getting them to say, 'We're going to give you money to help solve this problem,' which then solved the bigger problem," she says.

Before making customer experience a high priority in this transformation, product development was internally focused, centered around the technical team working on the software. But now, customer input helps inform the product development process, Singh says. "We have created applications specifically for human resources, legal and finance where we had none before and there are business customers now working with our developers to build on those platforms." All of these people inside and outside the company are now included in the communications from Singh's team.

Singh attributes part of the CX transformation success to the cross-functional cooperation for communications, business and customer-based prioritization of next steps, data sharing and product and service development. This in turn was invaluable for getting top executives to recognize challenges and opportunities and their support for those sizable and manageable next steps. "You can't transform everything at once, because there are so many different teams, and it's deciding what channels to change, and so much more," she says. This iterative approach has created an evolution of transformation that is compatible with customer goals—and those of investors too!

Before beginning a customer experience transformation you need an accurate view, qualitatively and quantitatively, of where your business is starting from, including levels of commitment; knowledge of customer experience best practices and related choices; sources of inside or outside objective guidance and training; and the ability to develop a detailed description of your present customer experience position worthy of an actionable starting point. (For more details about this see Chapter 6.)

Start-ups can build customer experience value at the outset and then evolve

The thieves got Björn Granberg's credit card information. He had a fairly good idea of when it happened, though not exactly how. These types of criminals sometimes use a small device attached to an ATM machine to skim the card information. Or they may have used a wireless scanning method while they seemingly innocently stood next to him on a crowded sidewalk. "Someone had taken money from my bank account. The bank told me I'd been to Russia and I had been gambling. I told them I haven't and don't gamble, I've never been to Russia," Granberg says.

Eventually, after filing a police report and proving that he hadn't been to Russia, he got his money back. While the episode "was not a pleasant experience," the theft of his data and his privacy and the time and effort it took to get his money back inspired Granberg and business partner Carl Martinsson to start their business SkimSafe in Europe and SkimSure in the United States.

One of the first things they did was take a careful look at existing market research to assess the volume of card-skimming and the fraud that goes with it. The hard numbers from the research validated that there was a business opportunity. The company, based in Sweden, was begun in 2016 and has sold over 400,000 products in the Nordic countries and the US. Last year revenues reached $7 million with 10 full-time employees. Their SkimSafe and SkimSure brands are growing in their respective regions, with major distributors including Best Buy and Walmart in the U.S., MediaMarkt in Europe and many big brands in the Nordic countries.

The company is profitable too. This early-stage profitability is attributed to watching their own investments in the business, being very customer-centric and using that customer knowledge to creatively communicate and connect with new customers about the company and their solution in all markets worldwide. But what exactly does being customer-centric mean to Granberg and Martinsson?

They have created a business culture of customer intelligence and customer experience. Granberg wants the customer knowledge—the numbers and words about and from the people who use their products—to guide him and the company. "We try to instill in everyone that we work with that it's completely irrelevant what my thoughts and feelings are ... if they're not connected to a customer. We're striving to make logical conclusions based on data about and discussions with potential and existing customers," he says.

While there is a person responsible for customer service, everyone in the company gets involved in answering customer questions, almost in a rotation. "It's part of everyone's job and it helps keep us in close contact with [our users]," Granberg says.

Another input to the company's customer intelligence portfolio is customer surveys. The goal is to be an experience maker—not merely aiming for satisfied customers but gaining insights to make improvements and innovations that will create active advocates. Starbucks and Apple are two of Granberg's customer experience role models. "Those big companies have a lot of customer ambassadors and people that love them and we've tried to show our employees how powerful that is."

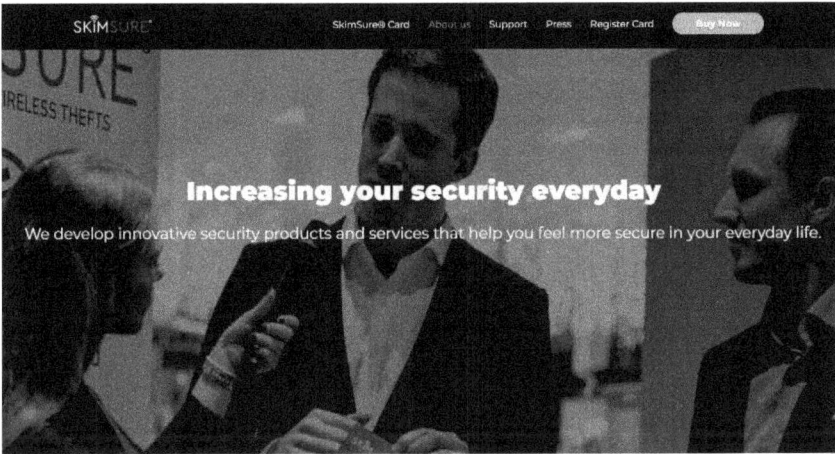

FIGURE 1.2 CX at SkimSure—what SkimSure does for customers. (Photo courtesy of SkimSure)

Anticipate customer needs and create a community feeling

Ultimately, the company's goal is to anticipate and innovate security solutions and experiences—even before customers are aware they need them. Not content to rely on technology and the momentum of early stage, high-growth markets for long-term value and differentiation, the job of the innovation Granberg describes is to create an ecosystem of products and services that deliver a personalized customer experience. "What we've been trying to do first is to create happy customers. We listen to them and we want to create a personal relationship with them so they feel this is not just another company. We need to do something beyond price, product or service features.

We need to have something more sustainable and valuable for the long term. A feeling about SkimSafe and SkimSure and Carl and me. A community feeling, where you feel like you're part of something bigger. Key to that is making the experience with us closer, more personal and more valuable. That's where we are going."

Insights at the train station

For Granberg, access to potential future customers is as close as the train station. He excitedly shares an example of how their ID-theft insurance product came to be: "We went to the nearby train station and started asking people, 'What do you think this product is? Do you understand it?'" These informal interviews and observations gave them quick data to take back to the office and make changes for multiple iterations. Then they would return to the train station the next day with an altered concept to run by potential customers.

Like many of the best in customer experience who have created long-term and highly sustainable growth and profitability, Granberg and Martinsson have combined their learnings from efforts like the train station interviews with other customer inputs and the macro data on market opportunities (when available).

For those thinking about focusing more or transforming the business to customer experience, Granberg offers some suggestions. "You need to set some kind of structure on how you do things and measure things and how you learn from your investigations. And then, based on that, you ask, 'Should I disrupt? Should I transform? What should I do?' Look at related trends and what your future and existing customers are saying and doing. Make a logical conclusion based on the data you have or will acquire to help decide."[14]

Transform to customer experience along a continuum

There are many different approaches to finding the customer experience focus and transformation that best serves your organization, customers and goals. The CX transformation continuum shown in Figure 1.3 provides a range of examples. On the left side are companies that decided to make the transition with consistent, multiple, incremental steps until complete. In the center are businesses that transformed to CX in sizable but manageable chunks. And on the right side are rare instances of businesses that made a big and bold transformation in a relatively short time.

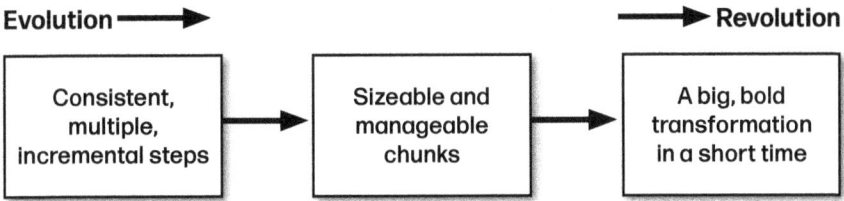

Evolution ——▶   ——▶ Revolution

| Consistent, multiple, incremental steps | ▶ | Sizeable and manageable chunks | ▶ | A big, bold transformation in a short time |

FIGURE 1.3 CX focus and transformation continuum.

Businesses choose where they are on the customer experience transformation continuum based on their actual CX starting point, competitive pressures, their leadership and culture, profit situation, business environment, urgency, how they value what is ahead for them and many more factors specific to their situation.

Being an experience maker is a valuable objective and is difficult for competitors to copy. Think of some well-known experience makers like Ally Bank, Amazon and USAA. Or newer, perhaps lesser-known companies like Everlane and Workday. Some started as experience makers while others transitioned to it. Most, if not all, have double-digit rates of active customer advocacy that increase revenue and decrease the cost of acquiring new customers and selling to existing ones. A very good position to be in.

The challenge for current customer experience leaders, early-stage businesses and existing organizations who are committed to being customer, patient or guest experience makers is to be relevant and valuable today and into the future. With product, service and company life cycles shrinking rapidly, the future could be as close as the next 12 to 18 months, depending on the market and customers you serve, related rates of innovation, low or high barriers to customer substitution, how sustainable your "better, different and profitable" status is and additional factors.

Understanding and anticipating the environment in which you need to operate and leverage is essential to being a next-generation customer experience leader.

Characteristics of next-generation customer experience leaders begin with a learned and then inherent understanding and appreciation of the value of customer experience to the organization—and the customer.

Future CX leaders are particularly aware of the uniqueness of the next generation as customers, users and influencers. People born after 1995, the generation known as iGens or Gen Z, are more different than any other generation in modern times. They came into a world where the internet was already here, its use ubiquitous and integrated into daily activities. Their experiences have shaped their development and expectations as customers, clients, guests and patients.

Having and using customer experience intelligence and related insights at strategic and tactical levels is vital. Those with intelligence about customer interactions that are prescriptive and predictive will have effective advantage over the competition. Those that have it in real time or near real time will have a decisive one.

> **Those with intelligence about customer interactions that are prescriptive and predictive will have effective advantage over the competition.**

Successful, profitable and sustainable customer experience-maker companies will leverage behavioral economics in determining, developing and delivering customer experiences and profitability. As we will explore later, decision-making based on behavioral economics offers a significant advantage over approaches based on old-school ways of thinking.

Next-generation customer experience leaders also use best practices centered around the development of customer experiences that garner increased customer advocacy and profitability. The samples of best practices in this book come from the authors' experiences, ongoing research and a select group of high-performing customer experience organizations.

While many entities develop strategies and tactics for businesses, sales, marketing, customer engagement and more, next-generation customer experience companies focus on developing strategies and tactics for customer interactions. Interactions with objectives of specific outcomes for customers, users and the business. Objectives based on timely insights derived from customer experience intelligence.

Our look at characteristics of next-generation customer experience leadership concludes with innovation. How it really happens and can happen for you and your company; key attributes of customer experience innovators. We take a careful look at what they do that makes them more effective at innovating than most others. And what they add to their customer experience intelligence that gives them a tangible edge in innovating next-generation customer experiences—an edge you can have too. That's what "Next Generation Customer Experience" is about!

Generation Z and their Customer Experience Revolution

Why it's essential to understand how different Gen Z is from all previous generations

"The breakneck speed of technology change has created a surprisingly large gap between those born in the 1980s and those who started life in the 1990s."

— Jean Marie Twenge, professor of
psychology, San Diego State University

CHAPTER 2 Overview

An introduction to Gen Z	The first generation born after the internet was here	The Gen Z approach to shopping	Surprise! Gen Zs still love to shop offline	The bottom line for customer experience decision makers

usinesses and managers take note: A new generation is arriving at your door and its members are diverse in their norms and unique in very important ways. Who are they? Gen Z, otherwise known as iGen, are opportunity creators for businesses. Companies need to understand that there are untapped opportunities to explore and appeal to them as customers. Creating engaging and pleasing experiences for the members of Gen Z, who are likely the future of your business, requires a specific and realistic under-standing of them to win their advocacy.

An introduction to Gen Z

iGen/Gen Z refers to the population born between 1996 and 2015, right after the Millennials. This generation has become the largest generation, constituting 32 percent of the global population—or 2.47 billion of the 7.7 billion people on Earth—surpassing the Mil-lennials and Baby Boomers, respectively.[17] Generation Z accounts for 20.5 percent of the U.S. population, behind Millennials (22 per-cent) and Baby Boomers (21 percent). Estimates say that by 2030, only 38.8% of the global population will be 24 years or younger, down from 41% in 2020.[18]

Compared to previous generations, Gen Zs are better educated. They are less likely to drop out of high school and more likely to be enrolled in college. Among 18- to 21-year-olds no longer in high school in 2018, 57% were enrolled in a two-year or four-year col-lege. This compares with 52% among Millennials in 2003 and 43% among members of Gen X in 1987.[19]

> **Gen Zs are digital natives with Internet-based technology being almost universal.**

Gen Zs are digital natives who do not know a world without smart-phones and Internet-based technology. Typically, their experi-ences—finding relationships, jobs, life-event celebrations—happen mostly online. Their early immersion in technology has brought a crucial difference in their mind-sets as customers, especially com-pared to any other generation. They have a new set of expectations and demand personalization of their customer experiences, largely driven by the variety of options and ease with which one can shop online. They are always on the lookout for flexible ways to interact with companies.

Unfortunately, the customer experience strategies of many companies are still tailored towards Millennials and earlier generations. These firms don't realize they are missing out on a completely new generation that is making a huge impact on society. This chapter focuses on customer experience from Gen Z's point of view, drawing from our experiences with them and from research including in-person interviews with Gen Z consumers conducted specifically for this book.

Businesses today are under constant pressure to live up to the expectations of their customers and provide an experience that caters to their changing needs.

The Customer Experience (CX) Effect

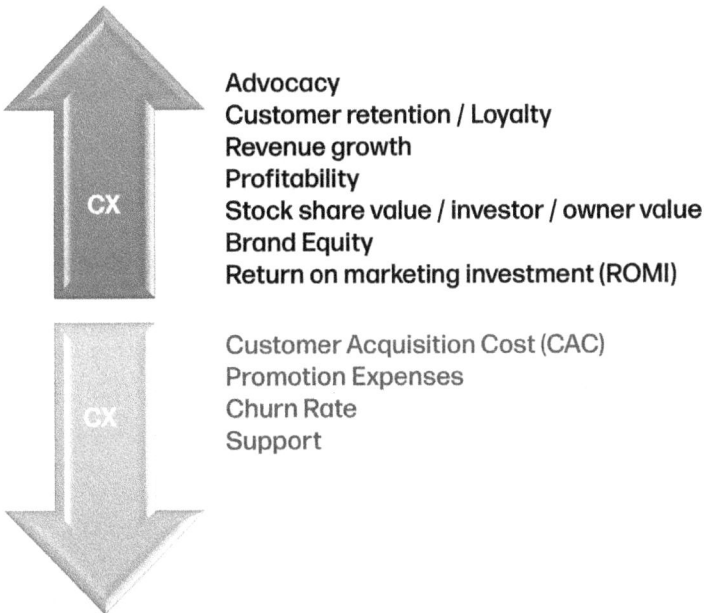

Advocacy
Customer retention / Loyalty
Revenue growth
Profitability
Stock share value / investor / owner value
Brand Equity
Return on marketing investment (ROMI)

Customer Acquisition Cost (CAC)
Promotion Expenses
Churn Rate
Support

FIGURE 2.1 The customer experience effect.

A positive customer experience fosters loyalty, helps with customer retention and creates customer advocacy. It also helps companies lower their sales/marketing costs and reduces stress related to operational infrastructure like support services, i.e., customer call volumes, emergency response plans. Companies should therefore focus on providing a positive customer experience, adapting to changes and delivering pleasing interactions that can inspire advocacy.

To stay competitive and provide a great customer experience, businesses need to keep an eye on trends and be willing to adapt in order to exceed expectations and turn customers into brand advocates. Leading experience makers set a purposely high benchmark and work towards retaining their customers and building advocacy. Apple, Amazon, Nordstrom, ServiceNow, Target and Trader Joe's are a few companies that win the hearts and money of multiple generations.

Gen Z—The first generation born after the internet was already here

> **Gen Z is the first generation that has never known a world without the internet.**

Experts say that Gen Z will not be an extension of the previous generation and should not be thought of as Millennials 2.0 but instead as a distinct set of people with unique experiences, beliefs and behaviors.[20] Therefore, companies need to work on giving them a positive customer experience, not just selling to them.

> **Gen Z should not be thought of as Millennials 2.0**

Immersed in the online world since birth, Gen Z surpasses Millennials in daily social media activity, with an average of 2 hours 55 minutes per day.[21] The smartphone is their preferred method of communication.

Many grew up playing with their parents' mobile phones or tablets and, on average, they received their first mobile phone at age 10.3 years.[22]

One way Generation Z differs from Millennials is their relationship to technology. While Millennials were early adopters of social media and smartphones, Generation Z has grown up with technologies and are often considered to be more reliant on them than their older counterparts.

Most Gen Zers are heavy users of many social networks to create connections, consume multimedia, play games and share content. Generation Z is likely to expect companies to be adaptable and flexible and use technology in innovative ways to improve the customer experience. Thus, businesses must make a high priority of marking their presence on social media and the internet.

Snapchat, TikTok and Instagram are the most popular social networks among Gen Z. Facebook, Pinterest, Twitter and Reddit also have relatively large followings among Gen Z.[23] However, there has been a recent shift in the number of Gen Zs using Facebook. Back in 2012, 94% of teens had a Facebook account, a Pew Research survey of 12- to 17-year-olds found. Almost 10 years later, only 27% of adolescents say they're on the platform, according to a 2021 survey of 10,000 teenagers conducted by Piper Sandler.[24]

Brands and businesses looking to connect with the Gen Z demographic on social media must have a thorough understanding of their social media habits and preferences. This includes the way they choose and utilize various platforms. For instance, we interviewed a 20-year-old male named Hunter from Utah, who is financially mindful and mature. He shared that he is heavily influenced by ads on Instagram and uses them as a means to discover new shopping locations.

In addition to discovering new places to purchase products and services, Gen Zs largely use social media to stay connected with friends and loved ones. Despite their embrace of social media for shopping and communication, Gen Zs are concerned about safety and privacy and prefer to post comments/feedback in public forums anonymously. Further, many are not comfortable sharing personal information for a tailored and enhanced customer experience, largely because they feel that their data is being misused by companies. Still, some are willing to sacrifice to get a positive experience.

Words can hurt as much as a physical assault.

It is common for members of Gen Z to have a heightened concern for safety, including the belief that words can be harmful and cause emotional damage. This can lead to increased sensitivity to written and verbal communication, as well as a desire to avoid potential conflicts or hurtful language. Many Gen Zers may also be more likely to actively seek out safe and inclusive environments where they feel comfortable and supported. This focus on safety and sensitivity can also extend to other areas of life, such as the use of technology and social media.

"[Gen Z's] interest in safety may be at least partially rooted in their long childhoods," says psychology professor Dr. Jean Marie Twenge, an expert in understanding generational differences and development. "When parents treat children as younger, they protect them more; generally, the younger the child, the less we let him out of our sight, the bigger her car seat and the more responsibility we feel for his or her safety. As 10-year-olds are treated like 6-year-olds, 14-year-olds like 10-year-olds, and 18-year-olds like 14-year-olds, children and teens spend more years fully aware that they are safe and protected in the cocoon of childhood."[25]

Thus, while chronological age may have served well as a benchmark for the preceding generations, businesses intending to serve Gen Z and give them a pleasing experience that inspires repeat purchases and customer advocacy must not default to assumptions about maturity based on age alone.

Gen Z—privacy matters

When we think of Gen Z, the first thing that comes to mind is how digitally savvy they are and how actively they participate in social media. But privacy matters a lot to this generation and they mostly like to use social media to stay connected with their friends and family, preferring to only share their experiences with their closed circles.

This generation utilizes social media as a way to keep track of influencers, become influencers themselves and gather inspiration based on their personal interests. They use social media to stay updated on the latest trends and get shopping ideas from influencers they follow. During one of our conversations, Kate, a Utah 10th grader, shared that she follows influencers on Instagram and if she likes something they have posted, she will look for where they purchased it and then buy it for herself.

When it comes to influencers, this generation is very careful about who they follow on social media. The vast majority follow people who care about the planet and make sustainable decisions. They also like to watch and follow influencers on YouTube. Most like to post pictures on Instagram based on their hobbies.

Suzanne, a motivated 23-year-old, mentioned that she uses Twitter to keep up with current events and news and she enjoys using Instagram to connect with her friends and follow influencers. Additionally, she follows individuals on YouTube and watches videos that align with her interests. Despite not posting videos herself, Suzanne is drawn to people on YouTube who are relatable and advocate for social justice issues. On Instagram, she frequently posts pictures of landscapes, her friends and family, sports and personal experiences. The content she follows on YouTube and Instagram often focuses on body positivity and family-oriented creators.

Aden, a thoughtful Gen Z from Los Angeles, expressed his privacy concerns when we asked him about virtual and automated assistants. "For personal privacy and security reasons, I don't use automated or virtual assistants because the technology is in the elementary stage but in the future, I might have to use it because there won't be a choice."

Customer experience should contribute and improve work life balance

Gen Zs have a real focus on their work-life balance. Compared to the previous generations at the same age, slightly fewer Gen Zs and late Millennials are focused on intrinsic rewards, such as an interesting job where you can learn new things and see the results of what you do. Many Gen Zs tend to switch jobs often if they are not happy with their current one.

It is equally true that as potential customers they will leave interactions that are not enjoyable, practical and safe. Across many years of teaching courses in advanced marketing and customer experience leadership at the University of California at San Diego, we've heard Gen Zs consistently comment, "If you don't give me a great user experience online, I will move on." To that same point, another oft-heard sentiment is, "If it's too many clicks, I am gone."

Gen Z and life goals

Gen Zs have a different approach to life and are often more independent and well-informed. Most of the Gen Zs we spoke to preferred to shop on their own. "I am an independent shopper and I tend not to prefer concierge service. I like to figure things out on my own before I ask for help," Suzanne says.

A distinctive aspect of Gen Z is their concern for their emotional safety, a point that is especially important in determining, developing and delivering customer experiences for them. It means assuring them that emotional risk is minimized when interacting with all parts of the customer experience continuum. This includes company or brand messaging, employees, processes and technologies and products and services.

The Stress in America 2020 report concluded that Gen Z adults rate their stress levels much higher than other age groups.[26]Thirty-four percent of Gen Zs said that their mental health was worse than a year ago compared to 21% of Gen Xers, 19% of Millennials, 12% of Boomers and 8% of those 75 and above.[27]

Ensuring positive emotional outcomes for each interaction with your business, from when people discover you to when they become customers and then, hopefully, advocates, is essential to bolstering initial and ongoing engagement.

Distractions—extra challenges for Gen Zs and businesses

People born into the internet generation are distracted and distractible—by things on the internet and things in the physical world. This is an extra challenge for businesses wanting to attract and engage Gen Zers. Your first and biggest competitor for their attention may be all the distractions around them. This is likely to vary by customer persona type. This puts more importance on customer intelligence and its freshness to understanding the different Gen Z persona types.

A persona represents a specific type of customer. Personas are used to help companies better understand their target audience and create products and experiences that are tailored to their needs, goals and behaviors. Personas are a valuable tool for companies, as they provide a clear and relatable representation of the user or the customer that can be used to guide decision-making and product design. By creating personas, companies can ensure that they are offering products and experiences that will be relevant and appealing to their target audience. Depicted in Figure 2.2 is the persona profile of Kiley, one of our interviewees.

Eco Friendly Kiley

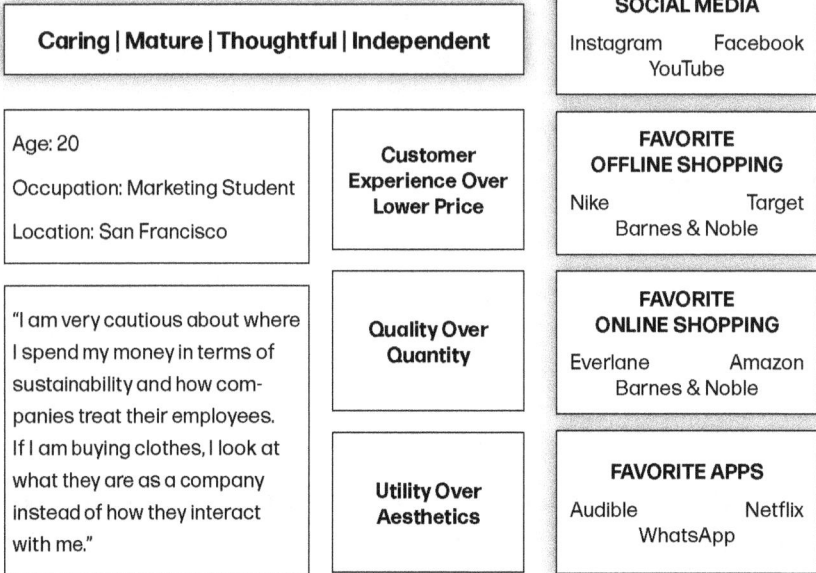

	PREFERRED SOCIAL MEDIA
Caring | Mature | Thoughtful | Independent	Instagram Facebook YouTube

Age: 20 Occupation: Marketing Student Location: San Francisco	**Customer Experience Over Lower Price**	**FAVORITE OFFLINE SHOPPING** Nike Target Barnes & Noble
"I am very cautious about where I spend my money in terms of sustainability and how companies treat their employees. If I am buying clothes, I look at what they are as a company instead of how they interact with me."	**Quality Over Quantity**	**FAVORITE ONLINE SHOPPING** Everlane Amazon Barnes & Noble
	Utility Over Aesthetics	**FAVORITE APPS** Audible Netflix WhatsApp

FIGURE 2.2 Customer Experience Buyer Persona 'Kiley'—Each element, or part of this CX buyer persona has been carefully included to help an organization better improve or innovate pleasing customer experience interactions for many customers like Kiley. The elements included may differ depending on industry, CX strategy project and interaction goals. The elements included may also vary if the persona is expected to be more prescriptive than predictive or the reverse.

Socially responsible generation

Gen Zs make informed judgments about the products and services they buy and the companies that sell them. They are socially responsible citizens with a much higher emotional connection to causes, particularly the environment and social justice. The widespread use of social media and other digital platforms has made it easier for this generation to access information about political issues and to engage in political discourse. This may be particularly true for Generation Z, who have grown up with these technologies and are comfortable using them to connect with others and share their views. Things like sustainability, saving the environment and giving back to society were commonly mentioned by most of the Gen Zs we spoke to.

Kiley, a 21-year-old marketing student who cares about her planet, says, "It is easy to be a heavy consumer and buy a lot of stuff without knowing if you will use it. People need to be aware of what they are buying and do their part to save the planet."

Molly, a student from Georgia, identified herself as socially responsible. "Most of the time, I stick to the same brand but I am willing to experiment between brands. I try to bring in an eco-conscious mind-set to my purchases and look for companies that give back to society."

Building trust with Gen Zs

Gen Z values integrity and places confidence in people they trust when making purchase decisions. Almost all the Gen Zs we spoke with said opinions and suggestions from friends and family have a major influence on their purchasing decisions. They also like to read online reviews before buying but are savvy enough to not blindly trust them.

"It is really important to read reviews because then I know I am getting a good-quality product," says Suzanne. "But there are always these outliers who post reviews because they are unhappy with the product so I take it with a grain of salt and do my research before buying. If a product that someone recommended to me has a low rating, I would read multiple reviews before buying it."

> **If we aren't given a great customer experience, or if a brand breaks our trust, we can easily move on . . .**

"We really do act on our emotions," Suzanne continues, "because if we aren't given a great customer experience, or if a brand breaks our trust, we can easily move on and collectively share bad experiences to social media or with our family or friend groups. Our customer advocacy of a brand or company, especially on social media, can go both ways: positive and negative."

However, many Gen Zs have less faith in online reviews. One possibility is that they have seen firsthand the potential for manipulation and fake reviews. With the rise of social media and the ease of creating bogus accounts, it's easier for businesses to post fake positive reviews or pay for people to post them. This can make it difficult for Gen Zs to know which reviews are genuine and which ones are not. Another reason for their lack of trust in online reviews may be the sheer volume of reviews available. With so many to choose from, it can be overwhelming and time-consuming to sort through them all and determine which ones are genuine and trustworthy.

The topic of trust—or lack thereof—also comes up in relation to Facebook, which most Gen Zs do not use due to privacy concerns. In fact, Facebook predicts teen use to plummet by 45% over the next two years, adding to a 13% drop since 2019, according to data obtained by The Verge. That data was found in part through internal documents leaked by Facebook whistleblower Frances Haugen to the SEC and earlier reported by The Wall Street Journal.[28]

Almost all the people of Gen Z we have spoken to, worked with or taught like to do thorough research before every purchase for products or companies they are trying for the first time. They prefer to make their own decisions and do not seek out a concierge service or other assistance unless it is something they can't figure out on their own or are pressed for time. In one of our discussions, Aden from Los Angeles told us, "For the most part, I like shopping on my own, but it also depends on what I am buying. If I am buying something expensive like a suit or a car, I would seek help from an experienced person rather than do it on my own."

Gen Zs are generally brand-conscious and are loyal to the ones they like. The most important factors they look for in a brand are quality and affordability—though they are also willing to spend more for high-quality, long-lasting products and better customer experiences.

The Gen Z approach to shopping

Gen Zs are used to getting instant outcomes, with companies like Amazon catering to their need to finish shopping quickly and get on to owning the product or having the experience. Businesses that provide an easy and stress-free shopping experience appeal to this generation.

Despite their youth, Gen Zs are not all driven by impulse when they shop. Many we spoke to take a careful approach, using browser plug-ins like Honey to hunt for coupon codes or online price-comparison sites or calculating the cost per ounce of products when shopping in-store. Companies and brands that understand this aspect of Gen Z consumers will have an advantage over competitors who do not.

Gen Z's focus is not on small acquisitions but rather on larger purchases such as houses, vacations, gift-giving, technology and related devices that have important do-fors. Do-fors are the practical benefits or functions that a product or service offers and Gen Z places a high value on them when making purchasing decisions, as they seek products that not only meet their needs but also improve their quality of life. They understand the value and benefits of a good customer and user experience, which in turn makes them willing to pay a higher price to get a smooth transaction. Companies, therefore, must focus on building a strong, customer-centric team and providing the kinds of delightful experiences that increase the likelihood of customer recommendations.

> **The marketing messages that engage and convert millennials to customers will not work on Gen Zs.**

Be inclusive and diverse. Gen Z is a generation that values diversity and inclusivity and they are more likely to respond to messaging that reflects these values. It is also important to be concise and to-the-point. Gen Z has grown up in a world where information is readily available and easy to access and they are used to receiving information quickly and efficiently. Therefore, it is critical to be clear and avoid using overly complex language. Overall, effective messaging for Gen Z requires a combination of authenticity, inclusivity, concision and visual appeal. By focusing on these factors, you can create messaging that resonates with this generation and helps you connect with them in a meaningful way.

Surprise! Gen Zs still love to shop offline

While Gen Z is the internet generation, they prefer shopping in stores in many situations, especially for products they are not familiar with. Kiley, for example, likes to combine offline and online shopping. "For convenience, with brands that I know are already my style and have my size, I would shop online. But if I am trying a new brand, I would go to the store and try it out because it is normally easier than ordering and returning."

Suzanne, on the other hand, prefers in-store shopping. "I like shopping offline because I can see and handle the products. Especially for clothes, it's easier for me to match colors and patterns."

Amazon—a favorite place to shop online

Gen Z loves shopping at Amazon for the same reasons so many other consumers do: convenience, low prices and fast, free shipping. But there are also instances where Gen Z feels the pain of small businesses that are impacted by Amazon's dominance. "In my opinion, Amazon is diabolical and I slow down on buying from them because of what they do to small businesses," Aden says. "But they are good at what they do. It is incredibly easy and fulfilling to buy from Amazon because you can browse, find what you want and it's at your doorstep in a day or two."

Kiley brought up Everlane, a clothing retailer based in the United States, as an example of how many people in this generation are shifting their support towards small businesses. She expressed her admiration for the company's mission statement, ethics and transparency. This highlights the impact that large retail giants have on small businesses and the growing trend of consumers prioritizing companies that align with their values.

Target—the most preferred place to shop offline

In our discussions, most Gen Zs named Target as their favorite place to shop offline. As with Amazon, Target's appeal spans generations and Gen Zs appreciate the venerable retailer's low prices, clean stores, broad range of products and excellent customer service—all factors that lead to a satisfying experience that shoppers are happy to relive again and again. They also noted that the uniform design of Target stores sets them apart from competitors and is more appealing. Target has always been successful in delivering a superior customer experience, making their stores popular shopping destinations for people across all generations. The use of bright colors and good lighting, along with a wide range of products, creates a welcoming atmosphere that makes customers feel good.

Along with Target and Amazon, the Gen Zs we spoke with mentioned many more stores as favorite places to shop, including grocers Andronico's and Trader Joe's, and clothing retailers Nordstrom and Zara. This generation values ease of shopping and a positive customer experience and will remain loyal to brands that consistently give them what they are looking for. For example, our Gen Z interviewee Jordan cited Andronico's, a California chain of community markets, as his favorite place to shop. "The staff there are helpful, they notice the needs of the customer and they provide a good customer experience," he says.

Pleasing customer experiences = increased customer advocacy

Customer experience is correlated to customer advocacy. When companies focus on excelling at every aspect of the customer journey, whether it's online and offline, shoppers take notice and become advocates.

In our discussions, the Gen Zs we spoke with placed a premium on customer experience over price. They believe in customer loyalty and always recommend their favorite places to shop to their peer group. They love to discuss their customer experiences and advocate for products, people and companies they like and enthusiastically use platforms like WhatsApp, Telegram and Instagram to share their experience with friends, followers and loved ones.

Automated and virtual assistants

Gen Zs are not comfortable using cloud-based devices or virtual assistants, largely for privacy and security reasons. Owning or understanding more about these devices is not a priority as they prefer doing things on their own and feel that the technology needs a lot of improvement. "I like the virtual assistants that are available online during the purchasing process that help me with certain things before I chat with an actual person," says Kiley. "I feel they are helpful. But when it comes to the cloud-based devices like Amazon Echo, I think they're creepy." In some aspects, this generation is still conservative and they believe and trust more in personal connections than devices and technology.

Devices

Based on our discussions with Gen Zs, it's clear that smartphones are the preferred device for browsing, shopping and communicating. On average, this generation uses their smartphone 80% of the time, with laptops coming in a distant second. Thus for businesses, websites and apps must be pleasing and efficient and companies must track and analyze insights about device-type selection and uses from their prospective and existing customers.

The bottom line

For customer experience decision makers, and all those whose work impacts customer experiences, whether directly or indirectly, it is essential to understand their Gen Z customers and the differing customer persona types that Gen Z encompasses. Customer experience strategies have typically been tailored towards the previous generations but because Gen Z is markedly different from the others preceding it, companies must switch gears and focus on developing a detailed understanding of these would-be customers, as this generation will comprise most of the population by 2030.

As we have outlined, Gen Zs are more focused on buying products from brands that align with their values. For businesses, this means they need to concentrate more on the attributes that align with and appeal to this generation, such as trust, quality and social responsibility. Companies that invest in and focus on delivering customer and/or user experiences that give Gen Z what it wants in a pleasing, efficient way will be relevant and valuable to them and more likely to be among the next generation of customer experience leaders.

Customer Experience Intelligence

Investing in a portfolio approach

"Shoemakers should be run by shoe guys, software firms by software guys and supermarkets by supermarket guys. With advice and support of their bean counters. But the final word goes to those who live and breathe the customer experience."

—Bob Lutz, who served as executive vice president and board member of Ford Motor Company, president and vice chairman and board member of Chrysler Corporation and vice chairman of General Motors

CHAPTER 3 Overview

What is customer experience intelligence? (CXI)	The customer experience four and the patient experience five	A customer experience intelligence portfolio including thick data	CXI input to insights to recommendation A small scale non-automated example	Advanced CXI for Next Generation Customer Experience

How do they do it? Time after time, the customer experience leaders—small or large, business-to-business or business-to-consumer—seem to have an inside track to understanding customers and pleasing them. This is not by accident. Most of the leaders have repeated success stories of determining, developing and delivering experiences that inspire people to advocate for them.

Is it some secret intelligence that is available only to them? Partly yes and partly no.

Yes, because companies have their own qualitative and quantitative data views just from being in business. No, because some of their methods of gathering customer experience intelligence can be used by almost any business.

These intelligence-driven customer experiences effectively make companies with well-developed and -applied customer experience intelligence (CXI) better and different for customers. They frequently lead in the discovery and effectiveness of new types of customer interactions by reducing the guesswork associated with profitable CX innovation.

These are just some of the hallmarks of a CXI-centric business compared to its non-CXI counterparts. CX leaders are committed to defining multiple inputs to feed their portfolio of information, which they convert to insights that enable effective customer experience decision-making.

What is customer experience intelligence?

CXI is the cultural and systematic combination of internal and external inputs from customers about all the interactions they have with your business, on the internet and off, directly and indirectly. It's about developing the capability to engage with customers in near real-time, capturing their feedback, both quantitative and qualitative, including structured and unstructured data, and then analyzing that stream of real-time data to generate actionable insights.

Customer experience intelligence allows you to get to know consumers in a deeper, more personal way with lifestyle information. The same is true for patients of health care organizations with the context of patient experience intelligence (PXI). For business-to-business firms, it means having deep insights about a customer's business, its goals, challenges and opportunities; its customer base;

and how you can help with your customer experience, including your messages, people, processes and technologies and products or services. When we've asked them to define early signs that their CXI efforts are working well, several experience-maker companies cite a much-improved ability to get potential and existing customers' time (and attention) and a measurable increase in customers relying on their organization and advocating for them.

Listening at scale to feedback and recommendations can align organizations to their customers' thoughts and feelings. This includes feedback about product quality, customer interactions and the organization's overall customer experience.

CXI also supports organizations in gaining insights that are not usually available in financial or enterprise planning and reporting systems. Customer relationship management systems include valuable data but often fall short of providing relevant insights driven by big-data analytics.

It starts with developing a deep understanding of customers, going beyond the traditional customer profile for your product or service. This contextual understanding allows you to apply the ingredients of customer experience in a way that leads customers and users to integrate your company's people, products and services into their life and their business.

CXI along the customer experience journey

There is a lot to know about customers. CXI yields implications for strategies, tactics, operations, current and future customer experience interactions and more.

This chapter is particularly suited to small to medium-sized businesses and to all organizations new to customer experience intelligence. The focus is on the interactions people have with your business, referred to here as interaction-level customer experience intelligence—something even many well-established large companies are missing.

> **An interaction is when two or more people or things (such as a laptop or phone with a business website or mobile application) communicate with or react to each other.**

What is an interaction? An interaction is when two or more people or things (such as a laptop or phone with a business website or mobile application) communicate with or react to each other. From a physical perspective, an interaction includes the transfer of energy between people or between people and the communication medium, such as the internet, pen and paper, a phone, a mobile app and a product. The environment in which people have the experience is also an important consideration for understanding it. The collective set of customer interactions[29] is what builds up the overall and dynamic customer experience.

The authors have worked with many businesses that do not understand the actual experiences their customers have with them. In these cases it's been extremely helpful to start by creating an internal view of the customer's experience at every interaction along their journey. We begin with discovery of the business and move through all the interactions of becoming a customer, including repurchasing, interacting with customer service and, in the best cases, becoming an advocate. The next stage is to define and evaluate an external view of interactions with the business based on customer experience intelligence.

Once you have evaluations of both internal and external views of the customer experience interactions, it's time to compare them and then consider what can be done to close gaps and improve or innovate interactions. For many organizations this is the beginning of their customer experience transformation. The point where customer experience is welcomed as part of the organization's leadership, culture and way of competing.

The customer experience four

Whether it's time, money or the day-to-day effort required to operate their business, all companies have constraints on their ability to transform information into insights for decision-making. So, what are the baseline types of intelligence we should gather about each interaction a person has with the company to make effective decisions about customer experience?

We call them the customer experience four or CX4. The CX4 is the minimum set of leading indicators to be understood for each interaction a customer has with the company, from the time they discover it to the day they become an advocate for it. With accurate information about each of the CX4 from various types of customers, decisions on improving or innovating specific interactions are more likely to be successful.

The CX4 includes

1) The value of the interaction
2) The range of emotions people experience while having the interaction
3) The customer perception of how the interaction used their time
4) The do-for/do-to—what the customer believes an interaction did for or to them

Since the same interaction could be experienced very differently by different customer types, it is crucial to understand the CX4 for each important customer persona. This includes paying customers, users who may not be the paying customer and the influencers of both.

CX4 #1 Value of the interaction

It is either during or after an interaction that a customer decides how good or not so good it was. How valuable was it for me, my family or my business? Did it cost me something in terms of time, pain, money, emotion or outcome? Was that call to the service manager worth it? Was my discussion with their industrial engineer about wind turbine bearing life expectancy valuable? Did the person I sent that e-mail to take me seriously?

CX4 #2 Range of emotions

While the value of creating positive emotional connections with your customers sounds obvious, many businesses do not take it seriously enough. The leaders in customer experience make it their goal to create positive emotional results for each interaction along the continuum.

Why? Because research has shown that delivering positive emotional outcomes may be the most critical factor in securing the ultimate value in a consumer or business relationship.

When a person has an interaction with your company, emotions are evoked. Whether it's happiness from having a problem solved by an online chat function or anger caused by a rude salesclerk in your store, the range of emotions a customer accumulates from interactions has an exponential impact on your business. These feelings will weigh heavily in deciding whether to have that interaction again or to make your company their go-to supplier in the future.

Donald Norman, founding director, the University of California San Diego Design Lab, former vice president of Apple Inc., and author of many books, including "Emotional Design: Why We Love (or Hate) Everyday Things," is a leading authority on emotion, design and business. He recounts that historically emotion has not been considered important. "It has really dominated Western thought and it dominates the training of MBAs today: that everything is by the numbers, everything is cool and rational. In fact, modern science, to say nothing of our intuitions, demonstrates such thinking is wrong. Those people who don't have emotions, and there are such people, can't make decisions."

Norman explains that emotions are value judgments. Deciding whether something is good or bad, safe or dangerous. No matter if you're buying a toaster or a fighter jet for the Air Force, there is a significant emotional component. "You would be surprised how these cool, rational Air Force generals make these decisions," Norman says. "They fall in love with the airplane. It does not matter what the facts say, they want that airplane. Um, $20 billion? I don't care. This is the plane for me. People who design these airplanes know that.

"It is all about the emotions you have. More important than the emotions you have, by the way, are the emotions that you remember. Because at the moment of the experience ... How long is it? It is an instant. It goes away. But in our memories, it is forever. And so, it is much more important that people walk away with positive impressions, feeling good."

A personal experience served as an instructive example of what Norman was talking about. I (Jeof) was the guest speaker at a gathering of the Orange County Product Managers Association and I was sharing my hopes and ideas for Best Buy to turn its fortunes around when a person in the audience stood up and interrupted me. "I hate those people at Best Buy," he said. I asked why. "I found a product I wanted on their website," he explained. "The site said I could order it online or buy it in the store. I went to the store. I could not find the product myself. I spoke to many Best Buy people. No one knew what I was talking about. I was embarrassed. We went online together to see what I was looking at. Finally, they found the product in the store, in the stock room, it looked a bit different and, worse, and it was for a much higher price. I refused to buy it."

The creditable detail, energy and outrage that this audience member expressed seemed fresh. Thinking this customer experience may have happened that evening on the way to the speaking event, I asked the man when it occurred. "Five years ago," he said. "I don't buy from them anymore."

Work and research experience prior to and since this incident has underscored that the emotions we remember are enormously powerful. Especially those leaving deep impressions of pain or pleasure, comfort or discomfort or unhappiness or happiness.

CX4 #3 Customer perception of time

This element of the CX4 is focused on the customer's perception of how the company used their time during an interaction. Unsurprisingly, people have a wide range of views about their time and how a business's people, products or services use it and it's crucial to understand them. Do potential and existing customers believe that their interactions with your company are time well-spent?

How your company and your customers value time can be quite different. When customer time and company time are aligned it increases the likelihood of repeat purchase and formal or informal customer advocacy.

CX4 #4 Do-for or do-to

No matter what type of interaction people have, they are concerned about what it does for them or what it does to them. And this is another instance where there is usually no middle. This has been found to be true in working with companies and health care organizations, in research and from the insights of the many customers and users interviewed for customer experience projects and three books.

For example, listen to people describe their past or anticipated interactions with their cable company or bank and it becomes evident that do-to is dominant. Customers of USAA, Workday and Turbo-Tax (Intuit) tend to recount or anticipate their interactions more on the do-for side.

In the book "The Customer Experience Revolution," we explained that do-fors are what products or services actually do for customers that they highly value. "They answer the questions: What will that do for me? and Why should I care? Delivering the do-fors well with an extraordinary customer experience can create advocates and additional revenue."[30]

Real do-fors go beyond traditional selling or value propositions to deliver interactions that please people to the point they are willing to pay with time, money or both—and likely become a customer advocate based on that one interaction.

Ask yourself: For your customers, does interacting with your messaging, your people, processes, products and services create do-fors or do-tos?

To gain insights on the CX4 about a customer's website purchasing interactions, we used in-person interviews and professionally conducted ethnography.

Internet	The CX4 of Customer Interactions	Quantified (-) 1............. 10 (+)	Qualified Words
	Emotional range	5	Intrigued and excited
Effective Customer experience intelligence (CXI) for an interaction of purchasing over the internet.	Value of the interaction	8	Great value, worth it for me
	Time spent Not well.....well	7	Quick. My time well spent
	Do for ... Do to	6	It was helpful

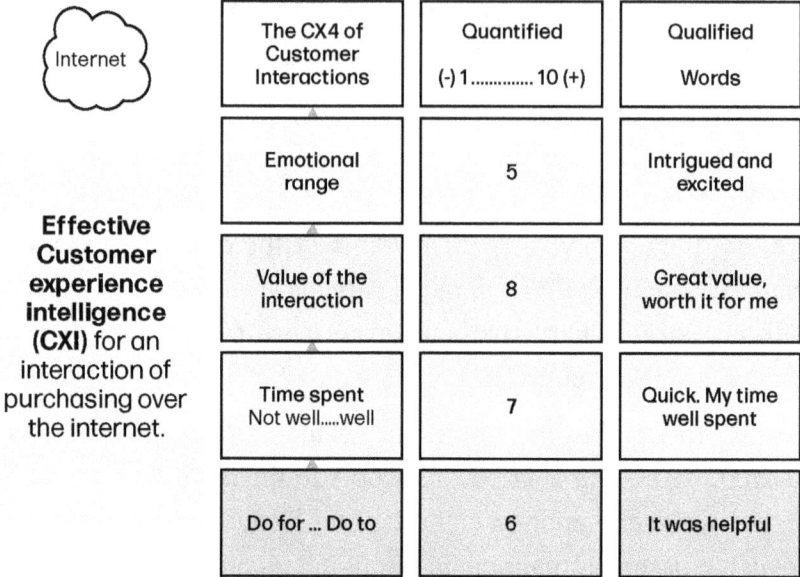

FIGURE 3.1 Summary results of a customer experience website purchasing interaction (second purchase) from an interview and ethnography.

During the in-person interview, a customer using the company's website to reorder products rated their emotions as a neutral 5 on a scale of 1 (felt frustrated) to 10 (felt accomplished). When this person described why they gave their rating as a 5, their words were more optimistic "between intrigued and excited." The value of ordering over the website was rated an 8 with the customer describing "great value." Regarding how the website used the customer's time, where 1 is time not well-spent and 10 is time well-spent, the customer gave a rating of 7, with the reason that it was, "Quick, [time] well-spent." Lastly, do-for/do-to earned a 6, with the explanation, "I feel better, energized."

The conclusion is that while the customer was pleased with their purchase using the website, there was room for improvement on the navigation, the use of colors and reducing the number of clicks to find and order products.

Adding a dimension—when the CX4 becomes the PX5

The minimum set of dimensions for each interaction can vary by industry. For example, in health care, the minimally acceptable categories of information about each (and all) patient interaction(s) are likely to include at least one more leading indicator: physical experience. Physical experience could include pain level, recuperation progress or many other dimensions specific to the context. Additionally, in health care, this is referred to as patient experience (PX).

The Patient Experience Five or PX5— Single interaction CXI example

Effective Patient experience intelligence (PXI) for the last injection in a six-month program to reduce swelling and eliminate pain in a wrist joint	The CX4 of Customer Interactions	Quantified (-) 1............. 10 (+)	Qualified Words
	Emotional range	5	Intrigued and excited
	Value of the interaction	8	Great value, worth it for me
	Time spent Not well.....well	7	Quick. My time well spent
	Do for ... Do to	6	It was helpful
	Pain - No Pain	9	Pain Free

FIGURE 3.2 Summary results of a patient experience interaction—the last injection in a six-month program to reduce swelling and eliminate pain in a wrist joint. Words and numbers from patient interviews and ethnography.

What 'completed' looks like

Take a moment to think about what a completed interaction evaluation form would look like for you. (Potential information inputs into the CXI or PXI portfolio will be discussed later in this chapter.)

Interaction name		> Discovery					Advocacy
Interaction number		>	1	2	>>>	14	15
Off internet	Interaction description– interacting with?					Receiving injection at Dr. office	
On internet	Interaction description– with/want to do?						
CX4 or PX5 Leading Interaction Indicators							
1 Value to customer 1 to 10	Rating number					8	
	Words Top 3 to 5					Quick pinch	
2 Emotional Range 1 to 10	Rating number					2	
	Words Top 3 to 5					Nervous, concerned	
3 Use of Time 1 to 10	Rating number					8	
	Words Top 3 to 5					Last Treatment	
4 Do For – Do To 1 to 10	Rating number					9	
	Words Top 3 to 5					Finally finished	
5 Physical Exp'ce 1 to 10	Rating number					10	
	Words Top 3 to 5					Pain free	

FIGURE 3.3 Partial view of the customer or patient experience interaction evaluation template tool. The blank spaces will be filled in with words and data from CXI/PXI inputs as in the patient interaction Number 14 above. The completed journey evaluation, based on inputs (findings) will be the basis of an end-to-end patient experience assessment specific to one patient type.

For instance, you have a customer or patient experience journey that has 15 interactions from discovery through advocacy. You have selected four or five dimensions (CX4 or PX5) for each interaction. This could produce minimally 60 to 120 pieces of information. It would be a solid start, particularly if it is the beginning stage of your organization developing and using customer experience intelligence.

Recently a project was directed where the entire customer journey, including all interactions customers had with the business, planned and unplanned, totaled over 60. Time constraints made it impossible to get high-quality insights about each of the CX4 on each interaction. Based on the history of the interactions and some current thick data on customers from inputs like in-person interviews, ethnography or internet interviews (more on thick data later in this chapter), we chose to focus on interactions 16 through 30, the thinking being that if we improved and innovated specific interactions in this set, we would be able to give the entire experience a positive lift.

Mind the gap—Compare internal views and customer views of interactions

Continuing to build your model, add words and number ratings from an internal perspective for the CX4 or PX5 about each interaction. Compare the results for internal and external perspectives. Were there differences? Why? Where do the internal and external views align well?

> **Like products and services, customer experience life cycles have stages of introduction, growth, maturity and decline.**

Refresh the customer experience life cycle

Insightful customer experience intelligence can help manage the customer experience life cycle. Like products and services, customer experience life cycles have stages of introduction, growth, maturity and decline. Timely decisions need to be made along the way to keep the customer experience relevant and valuable.

This is done with a view of the details that matter to people having interactions throughout the customer experience journey. Include the insights from the CX4 or PX5 and beyond. The hybrid portfolio of CXI insights also guides the best in customer experience to innovate new customer experiences including strategies and tactics for the overall customer experience and user experience within it.

Customer Experience Interaction Life Cycle
Position of a single interaction

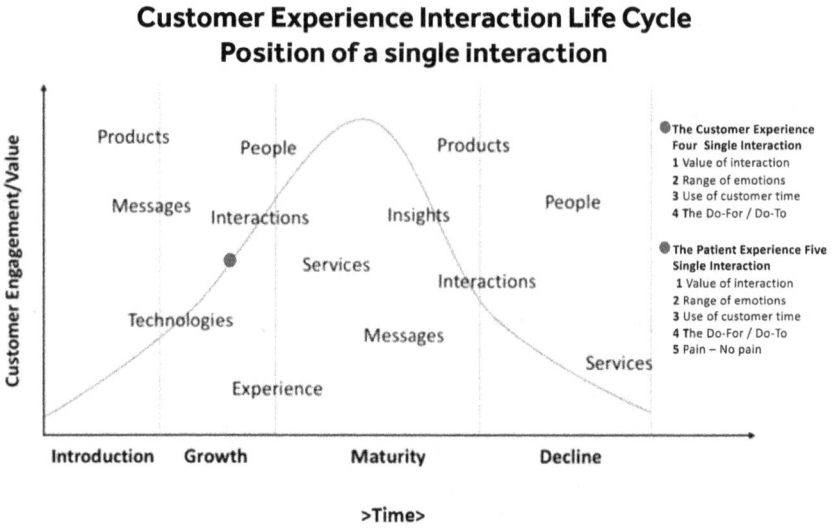

FIGURE 3.4 Customer experience interaction life cycle: single interaction. Like the life cycle of a product or service, the life cycle of a single customer experience interaction could be anywhere along the continuum of introduction, growth, maturity and decline. Where exactly depends on the value and relevancy of things.

The red dot shown in Figure 3.4 in the growth stage is the life cycle position of one interaction. The life cycle position of this interaction can change with time, with demand for it, with changes in customer behavior or advances in technology, etc.

The customer experience journey is made of multiple interactions and life cycles

A customer experience journey has a life cycle, one that is determined by customer interactions and their impact on the business and customers. Each of the interactions has its own life cycle and each may be at a different stage. Is the interaction in the introduction phase? Is its use growing? Perhaps the interaction has peaked in maturity and in its ability to create more sales, customer advocates and profitability. Or it may be declining in use, or worse, causing lost business.

Each interaction, whether online or offline, singularly and collectively contributes to the experience of the customer. And each interaction is made of the parts of the customer experience continuum. If a customer journey is made of 15 interactions and two of them are in a decline of their life cycle, are not relevant or valuable and/or perhaps off-putting to the customer, the entire experience is likely to suffer.

CXI inputs converted to insights about customer interactions across the entire journey will allow you to determine the life cycle stage of each interaction in the overall life cycle of the customer journey. It could be that just two of 10 interactions need some improvement and the entire customer experience life cycle would be lifted and create more profitability and advocacy. Or it may be that some interactions are beyond improvement and need serious innovating. In that scenario, the decision might be to start developing a completely new customer experience based on a set of improved and newly innovated interactions that will take the place of the present customer experience.

Where does customer experience intelligence come from?

Insights allow you to make better, more effective customer experience decisions. The aim of customer experience intelligence is to have a flow of insights that allows you to anticipate and innovate new customer experience interactions that will pleasantly surprise customers and cause them to advocate for you. Over time your goal is to be able to predict customer behavior. But where does customer experience intelligence come from?

Basically, it comes from unbiased information inputs from customers and select company resources about customer interactions. The CX4 and PX5 interaction examples are based on words and numbers about interactions from patient interviews and ethnography.

Why are we referring to words and numbers? In our experience working with companies and teaching students we've observed a tendency for people to exclude words as an important form of data and to think of information inputs solely in terms of numbers. But words, whether spoken or written/typed, are important. For example, if a customer gives an interaction a rating of 10 on a 10-point scale, it will be much more insightful if we can combine their rating with a written or verbal explanation of the reasons for that high score. This combination of words and numbers is often referred to as quali-quant—a pairing of the qualitative forms of marketing research (interviews, ethnography, etc.) with the quantitative (surveys, etc.).

The customer or patient interviews and observations were two of the many available information inputs selected to create the quali-quant data about the customer and patient interactions. For this evaluation, interviews and observations were an excellent choice for insights into the interaction experiences people were having. The number of information input sources, both inside an organization and from and about customers and patients, is growing, which is a good problem to have, especially if the selected information inputs, working together in a portfolio, help to later create insights for decisions impacting customer and patient experiences.

There are businesses that think numbers and words from customers or observations of them do not need interpretation to yield insights and are best handled by computers. This is a mistake. While it is fine to use automation for a portion of the process, it takes an analyst's thoughtful, objective input along the way to give a human context to the insights. This, in turn, helps improve the effectiveness of the decisions based on CXI about interactions and determining new customer experiences likely to create advocates.

At experience-maker companies, this process is ongoing and is combined with employees' day-to-day work on fixing, improving and innovating customer touchpoints.

An entire book could be written about customer experience intelligence and selecting the methods that are important inputs for a CXI portfolio. Here is an overview intended to give a high-level introduction to many of the formal and informal ways leading companies develop important knowledge about customers and their interactions with the company to increase their decision-making effectiveness.

Customers, Users and Influencers

Customers, users and influencers

Think carefully about your customers and how you define where your CXI comes from. Customers may not be the users of your products and services. When customers and users are not the same people, then customer experience intelligence needs to come from both.

For instance, an office or procurement manager may buy medical supplies for a doctor's office or hospital. They are the customer but the users will be the doctors, nurses and patients.

Influencers may be another source of customer experience intelligence and may be formally or informally a part of the purchasing process. Influencers can include colleagues, professional and non-professional reviewers of products and services in blogs, website articles and industry journals and magazines.

In certain markets, including influencers in your customer experience and marketing is vital to your ability to enter and be successful. Financial products and services are a particularly good example. A few years ago, *The Wall Street Journal* conducted a survey of their individual investor readers and found that 60% of them are influenced by and trust their financial advisors, reviewers and sources such as The Motley Fool, Money magazine, Morningstar and others. Less than 40% would go directly to the companies for information about products like mutual funds and other investment products. Having customers, users and influencers included in your intelligence portfolio of inputs gets you closer to having the best CXI effectiveness.

A Customer Experience Intelligence Portfolio

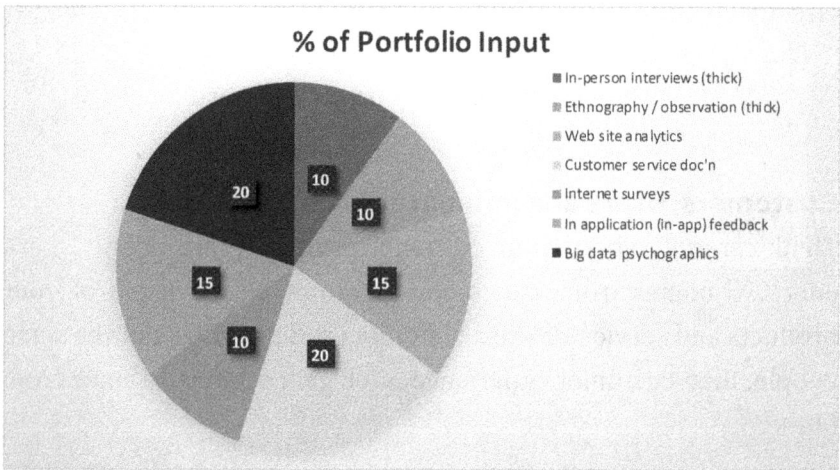

FIGURE 3.5 An example of the sources of information inputs that can be included in the customer experience intelligence portfolio. Having thick data from inputs like in-person interviews or ethnography, soon explained in this chapter, is an important partner with other input types for adding human depth and context to insights from the CXI portfolio.

A group of carefully selected inputs from customers, users and influencers is the basis for good CXI and the resulting insights and decisions. Keep in mind, though, that it may take some testing to get an effective, complementary combination of inputs (aim for a hybrid rather than a mongrel) to fuel the creation of beneficial insights.

You're not really listening unless you are willing to be changed by CXI

Your group of information inputs for customer experience intelligence can include listening, watching and accumulating qualitative and quantitative data. The success of the inputs depends not only on their quality but also on your organization's willingness to change and take action. Actor Alan Alda, a six-time Emmy winner, is also host of the podcast Clear+Vivid and founder of Alda Communications Training. Alda's definition of listening has tremendous meaning for organizations working with customer experience intelligence: "I have this radical idea that I'm not really listening unless I'm willing to be changed by you."[31]

Unless your organization is willing to take steps to improve customer interactions based on the insights that come from the process, you aren't really listening to customers and can't reshape the experiences they have with you.

The big, the thick and the usual suspects—CXI portfolio inputs

Companies on the leading edge of CXI have integrated the flow of intelligence into the organization in a consistent and dynamic way. It is part of how they work every day and what makes them successful experience makers.

There are many input methods for understanding customer experience. Whichever ones you choose need to fit into company culture, your budget and mesh with other available resources. You want to be sure to include sources that will give you a powerful combination of practical and innovative insights into the contexts in which people experience interactions. That means including thick data.

Thick data is information that comes directly from humans, with nothing in between. When properly combined with big data, internal data and other inputs not gathered directly from people, thick data is a focusing lens that helps create customer and user experience insights. It adds important nuance and color about how people experience interactions and makes information that is gathered about people, both qualitative and quantitative, relatable to humans.

Two sources of meaningful thick data are in-person interviewing (not to be confused with surveying) and ethnography. It starts out typically as qualitative and can have quantitative attributes attached to it.

Tricia Wang, an expert at developing business insights and effective results with ethnography and a fellow at Berkman Klein Center for Internet & Society at Harvard University, defined thick data in her landmark speech, "The Human Insights Missing from Big Data," as "data from humans, like stories, emotions and interactions that cannot be quantified." And, she added, "It comes in the form of a very small sample size but delivers an incredible depth of meaning." You are encouraged to watch the whole speech on YouTube.[32]

American writer Shelby Foote is the author of "The Civil War: A Narrative,"[33] a three-volume history of the American Civil War that took him several years to complete, as part of his mission was to capture the human context of the interactions of that conflict. While Foote did not use the term thick data, that is what he was looking for when he walked the former battlefields and closely examined the firearms, tools and conditions of those times to experience, as much as he could, the context of the long-gone people that he was writing about.

Foote knew the personal, professional and historical constraints of not having thick data, telling an interviewer years after the assassination of John F. Kennedy, "I don't think history will ever get any true view of John Kennedy and what he meant to us at the time he was alive, because the facts don't support what we felt.[34] Facts need thick data to give a more complete and contextual view of the human experience.

Thick data does not need to be large in scale to ground other types of inputs in the context and depth of a human experience. Think of it as a potent seasoning to be considered with other data and insight creation. High-quality thick data makes its contribution when it is objectively integrated with these other types of data to help give insights in a combination that includes context and human dimensions such as emotions, do-for and do-to and the perception of how time is used in an interaction.

Integrating thick data with other types of information increases the likelihood that a more exacting narrative pattern or set of insights around human interaction will be revealed, answering the questions: "What's the story [and outcome] with this type of person and that interaction? And why?" By including thick data, the narrative pattern will reveal points and insights that otherwise would be missed.

Don Norman helps us understand why thick data is so important to combine with non-thick data: "We need both the formal process of logic and the soft, subjective impressions from everyday experience."[35] He also emphasizes that, "Logic is not a good model of human cognition." Thick data adds available insights to non-thick data about a person's mental processes for acquiring knowledge and understanding through thought, experience and the senses. Norman explains that people are good at many things including language, music, poetry, invention, feeling joy, love and excitement. "But these are not the humans that technology sees."[36] Thick data illuminates these attributes and others that are vital to the human experience and helps us understand the customer.

Examples of information choices for CXI portfolios

Here are some examples of information sources or inputs that companies may use in a portfolio of qualitative and quantitative inflows that can be converted to customer experience intelligence.

Note that this list of examples is divided into thick data and non-thick data. Only a small subset of the companies that use thick data combine it with non-thick data types to get customer insights to their decisive advantage.

Thick data sources

- **In-person interview.** The person being interviewed is asked specific questions, professionally created to develop insights for customer experience decision-making by the interviewer while they sit together.
- **Internet interview.** The next most effective method to in-person interviewing is doing the interview in a video session such as Zoom, Skype or FaceTime, where the people doing the interview can see and hear each other at the same time. A voice-only interview is not a substitute, as it does not include the visual information for the interviewer during the interview.
- **In-person ethnography.** The business world has borrowed this technique from sociologists and anthropologists. Ethnography is a research method using hands-on, on-the-scene learning and it is relevant wherever people are relevant. It requires blending into and observing a population of people you want to learn about. You can also observe people ethically and unobtrusively while they are interacting during customer experiences and user experiences.
- **Focus group.** A focus group is a marketing research tool in which a small group of people (typically eight to 10 people) engages in a roundtable discussion of selected topics of interest in an informal setting. The focus group discussion is usually guided by a professional moderator. It is listed last here as it can be a good supplement method to the other thick-data inputs if done in an unbiased way and with minimal intergroup opinion or reaction interference.

Non-thick data sources

- **Artificial intelligence or AI**—applies advanced analysis and logic-based techniques, including machine learning, to interpret events, support and automate decisions and take actions[37].

The name AI can be misleading. "I think AI is somewhat of a misnomer," says Daron Acemoglu, an AI economist at Massachusetts Institute of Technology. Acemoglu tracks AI technologies, applications and their economics and has a more grounded description of what AI is and does: "AI uses massive amounts of data to turn very, very narrow tasks into prediction problems." AI researchers say that with enough data, they can train their algorithms to do very specific tasks.[38] AI is on an accelerated pace for creating and combing multiple narrow tasks to take on wider and wider tasks.

One of the many wider tasks is the fast-growing capability of customer experience intelligence. Federico Cesconi, CEO and co-founder of Switzerland-based SANDSIV Customer Intelligence, emphasizes the growing ability of AI to contribute customer insights at companies this way: "If data is the oil of the future, people's ability to generate insights must be democratized: AI allows you to interact with data in your native language. Create insights quickly without being a data scientist."

- **Cognitive analytics**—machines learn from experience and analyze data to identify associations. Inspired by human brain learning processes.
- **Cognitive computing**—combines artificial intelligence and machine-learning algorithms to reproduce data that mimics human thinking.
- **Conversational artificial intelligence or chatbot(s)**—set of technologies of automated messaging and speech-enabled applications offering human-like interactions between computers and humans.[39]

- **Customer experience analytics**—the systematic discovery, collection and analysis of customer data to gain intelligent insights to improve or innovate customer experiences.
- **Customer experience management**—designing information systems and reacting to customer interactions to meet or exceed their expectations.
- **Customer idea portal**—welcomes verified customers to securely share their ideas with the company and with other customers.
- **Customer relationship management (CRM)**—a software data system for managing a company's interaction with current and potential customers.
- **Customer support and customer service documentation**
- **Dark data**—the information assets organizations collect, process and store during regular business activities but generally fail to use for other purposes.[40, 41]
- **Data analytics**—qualitative and quantitative techniques and processes used to enhance productivity and business gain.
- **In-application (in-app) feedback**
- **Internal data**—information created by the operation of an organization; includes sales, purchase orders, transactions in inventory and customer interactions.
- **Machine learning**—an application of artificial intelligence that gives systems the ability to automatically learn and improve from experience.
- **Natural language processing**—a branch of artificial intelligence that helps computers understand, interpret and manipulate human language.[42]
- **Online surveys**
- **Paper-based surveys**
- **Predictive analytics**—use of data, statistical algorithms and machine learning techniques to identify the likelihood of future outcomes based on historical data.

- **Prescriptive analytics**—recommends the best course of action when making complex decisions involving trade-offs between business goals and constraints, using optimization techniques.[43, 44]
- **Telephone interviewing**
- **The Internet of Things**—refers to the connection of devices (other than typical devices such as computers and smartphones) to the internet.
- **Unstructured data**—data that doesn't fit neatly in a traditional database and has no identifiable internal structure.
- **Website analytics**

These are some examples of the many possible sources of information input flows to consider as part of a customer experience intelligence input portfolio. There are few thick-data options compared with non-thick data options. A CXI portfolio with a carefully selected combination of thick and non-thick data inputs including, but not limited to, the customer interaction level will also create insights for customer experience strategies. New input sources will continue to be discovered and tested. For example, the ability to analyze the text of social media posts for prescriptive and predictive insights.

Measure what matters to your customers—Dr. Gardner's rule

One of the most important questions asked by people committed to customer experiences is: What should I measure to make the biggest improvement for my customers now or if I want to create a new customer experience? The answer: Measure what matters to your customers, says Dr. Joely Gardner, Ph.D., CEO and chief user researcher at Human Factors Research.

While measuring what matters to your customers may sound obvious, "The truth is that few companies actually do it. This opens a tremendous opportunity for companies that will invest the time to find out what the measures should be and do it," Gardner says. She cautions against depending solely on the easy-to-count metrics. Instead, typical key performance indicators (KPIs) focus on business economics, acquisition and retention.

Examples of easy-to-count metrics

- Number of customers retained
- Percentage of market share
- Dollar value for new customer contracts signed per quarter
- Percentage of website visitors converting to customers

Measures that matter to customers

- How much time will this laboratory management software save me in locating frozen lab samples stored globally for additional analysis?
- After my suit or blazer is in the suitcase for 12 hours, how much time will it take after hanging to be wrinkle-free?
- How long will it take for a customer to receive a response from the chatbot?
- If I complete this "contact us" form on the shoe company's web site, how long will it take to get an answer?

Although some KPIs may impact customers, they mean much more to the company. "These items are not unimportant. They are not the things that contribute most heavily to pleasing the customer for a positive experience. You have a limited time with your customers, don't waste it on [internal measures or other sources] you can get on your own," Gardner says. "Focus on measures that are meaningful to customers."

To determine which measures matter most to customers, you need to do in-depth interviews. Following those interviews, you can include a review of help-desk records, particularly complaints, social media comments and discussions with salespeople. You need to listen to what people believe the issues are and what is important to them. Is something missing from the present experience? Is there something you should remove?

Gardner feels strongly that you need a combination of qualitative information and quantitative data. "I love numbers, numbers are great. But numbers never tell you why. You absolutely have to have the interviews on why they give an item a particularly high or low rating." Surveys with fill-in text blocks that ask people to include reasons for their selection can be helpful, depending on your customers' willingness and ability to be precise about the cause of their angst or source of delight. Yet surveys are not a replacement for interviews.

While interviews are a valuable tool in determining what is important to customers, people can be preoccupied with what is in front of them and focused only on improving what they can see or think about at the time. Following up later with customers to have them use a prototype of the product, service or interaction experience based on their prior input can help verify the direction of the development. It can also be an opportunity to test new measures that customers previously indicated they care about.

That is where some thoughtful anticipation and creativity can be combined with interviews or other methods of research. Steve Jobs exemplified this when he was asked if Apple conducted consumer research on the iMac when it was developing it. "No. We have a lot of customers and we have a lot of research into our installed base. We also watch industry trends carefully. But in the end, for something this complicated, it is really hard to design products by focus groups. A lot of times, people do not know what they want until you show it to them. That's why a lot of people at Apple get paid a lot of money because they're supposed to be on top of these things." The same is true for deciding what measures matter most.[45]

Businesses of all sizes and growth stages can combine meaningful interviews with thoughtful anticipation and ingenuity to develop the measures that matter most to customers. Discovering and creating them is a critical part of customer experience innovation.

Transitioning data, observations and words to insights

For small companies—say, those with less than 50 employees—customer intelligence still matters and it is worth the time to get valuable feedback on all aspects of the customer experience. But these businesses, due to their size and a presumably lesser degree of internal complexity, may not need to employ large quantitative models and systems for this purpose. Software-as-a-service (SaaS) products including CRM systems or customer/stakeholder engagement systems might still be useful and they are relatively inexpensive.

Medium-sized companies with more than 50 employees and a customer base in the hundreds need to think about CXI in a more serious way, not only to gain and retain customers who will be very pleased and likely to advocate but also to ensure sustainable competitive advantage and profitable growth.

The goal of transforming customer data, words, visuals and other inputs is to create insights. Insights might stand alone as the basis for decisions or be combined with prior efforts and innovation success for effective customer experience development.

Ultimately, with a combination of thick data and non-thick data about interactions flowing into the company you will have insights to help make effective decisions about the factors that influence the customer's experience.

Below is an example of a transition to insights. It would work well for small to medium businesses or even for large companies just starting out with customer experience intelligence. It is especially applicable to businesses working on their initial view of what the customer is experiencing.

Many companies, further along, have their CXI processes assisted by automation for efficiency. But for learning and for quality, people need to be involved in most parts of the transformation from inputs to insights stages so that human attributes are not lost. If the process is left completely to machines, much of the value of thick data will be filtered out.

CXI input to insight to recommendation transformation stages

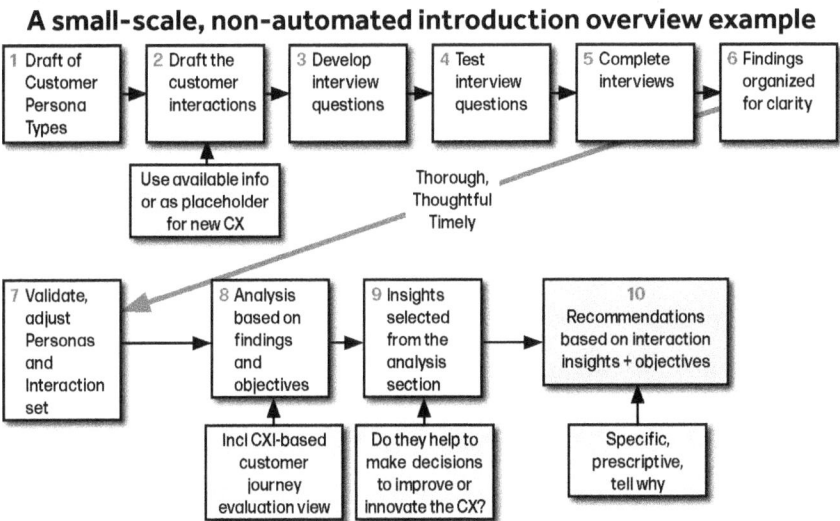

A small-scale, non-automated introduction overview example

1 Draft of Customer Persona Types	2 Draft the customer interactions	3 Develop interview questions	4 Test interview questions	5 Complete interviews	6 Findings organized for clarity

Use available info or as placeholder for new CX

Thorough, Thoughtful Timely

7 Validate, adjust Personas and Interaction set	8 Analysis based on findings and objectives	9 Insights selected from the analysis section	10 Recommendations based on interaction insights + objectives

Incl CXI-based customer journey evaluation view

Do they help to make decisions to improve or innovate the CX?

Specific, prescriptive, tell why

FIGURE 3.6 Customer experience intelligence information input to insight to recommendation process stages. A small-scale, non-automated introduction example.

Objectives for this overview example:

- Document specific qualitative and quantitative understanding of the customer experience journey evaluation at each interaction point (the CX4): 1) the value of the interaction; 2) the range of emotions people experienced; 3) customer perception of how interactions used their time; and 4) do-fors along the customer journey that real customers have experienced.

- Make specific recommendations for each interaction to keep as-is, fix, improve or innovate and why. What will the recommendation do for the customer and the business?

1) Draft the customer experience buyer persona types by selecting the elements to include in the persona profile that CXI inputs will help to complete. The business-to-consumer persona is page one in Figure 3.7. For business-to-business customers, page two is added to page one. Page one is about the business persona type being interacted with and page two is about the business.

Start with existing information and validate or adjust the persona profile with CXI including thick data. Or start with CXI including thick data and create the personas.

B to C
Persona name here
Text summary here (at a glance)

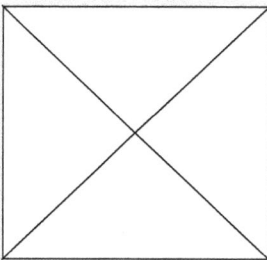

Photo:

"Personal or Professional Mantra"

Do-Fors
"Best things people, processes, products or services can Do For me"

Opportunities

Challenges

Business or social causes

Urbanicity   Demographics
Age:
Gender:
Marital Status:
#/Age of Children:
Location:
Occupation:
Job Title:
Annual Income:
Level of Education

Household or Business Technology
      (Below avg to Above avg)
(Postal) Zip Code: (for adding big data)
Car   Lifestyle and media traits
Restaurants
Shops online at
Shops off Internet at
Non-at-work activities
Buying process
Vacation activities
Vacation travel locations
Favorite airlines
Uses social media
Influenced by social media for purchases
Influencer of social media for others purchases
Listens to / music type
Watches types / programs examples

Notable lifestyle, media, buying traits	Stays smart (effective) and informed by
	Preferred devices to access Internet
	Preferred application 1 and for what
	Preferred application 2 and for what
	Preferred application 3 and for what

B to B supplement
Company name here
Industry
Market share
Profit margins compared with industry
Competitors
Leadership
Leadership culture
Metrics of performance (KPIs) internal / external
Economic trends
Formal or informal buying process
Buying process details and requirements

Top industry opportunities

Top company opportunities

Top industry challenges	Uses social media (business specific)
	Influenced by social media for purchases
	Influencer of social media for others purchases
	Listens to podcasts by
	Watches types / programs examples
Top company challenges	Stays smart (effective) and informed by
	Preferred devices to access Internet
	Preferred application 1 and for what
	Preferred application 2 and for what
	Preferred application 3 and for what

FIGURE 3.7 A buyer experience persona intelligence development template tool, page one of two (page one business to consumer; add page one to page two for business-to-business). As presented to the International Leadership Association (ILA).[46]

2) Draft the customer experience interactions using available information and correcting or adjusting after getting CXI inputs. In this overview, we have interviews with customers. If interactions are unknown or CX is all new, begin with CXI and complete with the results.

Interaction name		Discovery	TBD		TBD	Advocacy
Interaction number	>	1	2	>>>	14	15
Off internet	Interaction description– interacting with?					
On internet	Interaction description– with/want to do?					
CX4 or PX5 Leading Interaction Indicators						
1 Value to customer 1 to 10	Rating number					
	Words Top 3 to 5					
2 Emotional Range 1 to 10	Rating number					
	Words Top 3 to 5					
3 Use of Time 1 to 10	Rating number					
	Words Top 3 to 5					
4 Do For - Do To 1 to 10	Rating number					
	Words Top 3 to 5					
5 Physical Exp'ce 1 to 10	Rating number					
	Words Top 3 to 5					

FIGURE 3.8 Interactions evaluated with a customer interaction evaluation template tool and later populated by the findings from the CXI inputs before the analysis. This interaction journey was best evaluated with a linear template to capture first-time buyer likely chronology. Notably, buyer interactions can be non-linear and the same is true for the crossover between and simultaneous use of off-internet and on-internet interactions. This is a partial view of the top part of the template.

3) Develop interview questions. The mission of the interview questions is to get enough quantitative and qualitative detail from customers about the interactions they have with the business at the CX4 level (or PX5 level for health care interactions) for analysis that can create insights that will help make effective decisions to fix, improve and innovate interactions and experience strategies.

4) Test the interview questions. Use an agreed-upon number of in-person interviews to test the results of the questions for detail and insight potential in the answers. Adjust questions as needed to receive a helpful, unbiased level of detail and insight potential in the answers. See more helpful information in the Step 5.

5) Complete the interviews. Interviews should be done in-person or by using Zoom, Skype, FaceTime or other virtual application. Since interviews are a key input to getting thick data, they must be direct interactions so you can see and hear who you're interviewing in real time. For non-video interactions, be sure to audio-record the sessions with the permission of the interviewees, informing them up front that the recording is confidential, never to be posted online and will be used for notes and possible transcription to text. An audio recording can be listened to or transcribed into text (from a transcription service) after the interview. This can partially or completely relieve the interviewer from having to take notes. It increases the likelihood they can focus on the interviewee, head up and face-to-face, with the goal of having a flowing discussion including the questions. The recordings also serve as anonymized audio references and confidential proof of customers' views to help support the case for improvements or innovations.

6) Organize the findings. The goal is to have the answers, numbers and words associated with each question from all people interviewed in one organized area. Depending on the number of answers to each question, this can give an at-a-glance view for making the next steps easier for the person in this example, where they are doing the work manually using Word or Excel rather than using a CX software platform. This is the least fun part of the process as the findings are created by transferring them into a visual format for clarity from recordings or text transcriptions. Here is an example of one of the formats that shows the results for an interaction—Interaction 7, Question 5, with answers from four people and two persona types, P1 and P2.

Int #7	Quantitative	Qualitative
Q 5	How well was your time used when you arrived at the shop for service?	
5a	1 Not well used <1 2 3 4 5 6 7 8 9 10 >Very well used 10	5b Why did you rate it that way?
P1a	8	Quick in, fixed and out.
P1b	7	OK. Waiting area needs more AC outlets.
P2a	6	Waited 5 minutes until I was greeted.
P2b	9	Made appointment using the app, they took me right away.

FIGURE 3.9 The goal of a format for the findings (a manual entry, small-scale example) is to have the answers (in numbers and words) to each question from the different customer persona types to create an at-a-glance view. Formats vary widely depending on the combination of information inputs, scale and degree of human involvement.

Using Software for Large-Scale Integration of CXI

For integrating customer experience intelligence on a large scale, beyond the important hands-on learning example here, there are various customer experience software and software-based platforms. Some of the larger companies providing software or software platforms are Qualtrics, Medallia and Teradata along with many smaller and newer companies evolving data collection and analytics capabilities.

The best will create interaction experience intelligence from end to end in the customer journey, on and off the internet, quantitatively and qualitatively. Some gather only data while other providers claim that their software creates actual insights to improve and innovate customer experience.

While an evaluation of the vast number of software or software platform choices available is outside the purpose of this chapter, be sure to add the following in your assessment beyond cost:

- Determine where the automation begins and ends
- Obtain business and customer use cases
- Assess the ability to test on a small scale before fully committing
- Does it offer a graphic representation of all interactions and summaries of associated updatable qualitative and quantitative data?
- How is quantitative and qualitative thick data compiled?
- Does the platform provide insights creation?

- The expense, technical challenges and time required to switch to alternatives
- Time and expense of training users
- Does it offer dynamic scaling with the needs of customers and the business?
- Does it offer the ability to help the organization go beyond customer satisfaction and improve measurable customer advocacy?

7) Complete the template tool. Next, the findings are used to validate and adjust what is known about the personas and complete the customer journey evaluation template tool (example in Figure 3.10), one for each customer persona type, including answers about the CX4 or PX5 leading interaction indicators. This truing-up based on the findings will help tell the story in the analysis of which interactions are working and for which customer personas in the next step.

Attention to accuracy and completion at this step (7) is very important as it is the foundation for the next step, writing the Analysis of each interaction. Interactions analyzed while accessing a completed Findings template and a subsequent update to the customer persona(s) and completion of the customer interaction evaluation template tool allow for a much more effective analysis (see Fig. 3.11 for examples).

Later in this process, the analysis and the resulting insights will be the foundation for recommendations and decision making at the CX strategy and interaction levels.

Interaction Name / Interaction number		Discovery 1	Consideration 2	Visit the Shop 3	After Purchase 8	User Experience 9	Advocacy 10
Off Internet	Interaction type	Discover new trends and inspiring styles	The decision immediately goes to ChanX. No decision based on general product category but only on a high brand awareness towards ChanX. Information search about ChanX products. (First brand decision, after that the product overview)	Visit to the Chapel store in Munich, especially kept a whole day free for this visit, big welcome	> Exit the store and "Goodbye"	The user experience with the service and the product is evaluated by the customer	Customer has the opportunity to become a brand ambassador and share experiences
	Interaction description	Inspiration and discovery: People on the street, ChanX store, Friends, Shopwindows	Active exchange and high emotional involvement: ChanX store, Friends	Security at the beginning. Sales assistant is waiting directly in the store	> Champagne is offered last, Sales assistant escorts to door and says goodbye, official conclusion of the in-store experience	The purchase and user experience is evaluated.	Proudly carry the product in public and tell about product and experience
On Internet	Interaction type	Discover the new trends and styles worldwide	The decision immediately goes to ChanX. No decision based on general product category but only on a high brand awareness towards ChanX. Information search about ChanX products. (First brand decision, after that the product overview)	Opens the own website of Chapel from the laptop at home	> Purchase is confirmed, E-Mail is sent with the confirmation and details of delivery	The user experience with the service and the product is evaluated by the customer	Customer has the opportunity to become a brand ambassador and share experiences
	Interaction description	Inspiration and discovery: Social media (Snapchat + Instagram + TikTok + Twitter), Brand communities, Blogs, Online magazines (Vogue)	Active exchange and high emotional involvement: Marketplace, Brand community, Social Media, Specific Apps, Blogs, Magazine, ChanX website	Direct input of Chapel in the "search bar".	> Personalized email, click on the invoice and live tracking	The purchase and user experience is shared online with acquaintances, friends and family, including photos / videos of the product. Social media includes Snapchat + Instagram + TikTok + Twitter.	Report the experience via texting and on the Internet and share content (including videos and photos) about the product. Social media includes Snapchat + Instagram + TikTok + Twitter.

FIGURE 3.10 Interactions evaluated with a customer interaction evaluation template tool (partial view) and later populated by the findings (as shown) from the CXI inputs before the analysis creating an intelligence-based view.

8) Analyze the data. The analysis tells the story of each interaction and what is working and not working and why for each customer persona type. It is based on and should include the numbers and words from interviews with customers about each of their interactions. The analysis is written based on the findings and CX project objectives with the access to the updated customer persona types and a completed customer journey interaction evaluation template (see example in Figure 3.11).

Be sure to write the analysis for each persona and each interaction:

Persona 1a Customer journey interaction analysis:

- Interaction 1
- Interaction 2
- Interaction 3
- Interaction 4 Mobile app Product Selection—Ease of finding what you are looking for.
  This interaction was about the ease of finding the desired items and adding them into the shopping cart.

  On a scale of 1 [not easy] to 10 [very easy], persona 1a rated this interaction a 6 finding the product search and selection "kind of easy."

  There are many filters on the app that can be used according to customer preferences while selecting the products. Persona 1a mentioned that "even if all the filters are used there are still too many products to choose from the results. This can be confusing and time consuming." The . . .

- Interaction . . .
- Interaction 11 Advocacy . . .

Interaction Name Interaction number	Discovery 1	Consideration 2	Visit the Shop 3	After Purchase 8	User Experience 9	Advocacy 10
Leading Interaction Indicators						
1 **Value to customer** 1 to 10						
Rating number			Range: 7-10			
Words Top 3 to 5			>	>	>	
2 **Emotional Range** 1 to 10						
Rating number			10	>	10	10
Words Top 3 to 5	Inspire, up-to-date	Only one option, clarity, excitement	Excitement, exclusivity, glamour, reliable, charming	> Overwhelmed, happy, "feel-good-treatment"	Loyalty, unique, experience	Big family, exclusive, proud, self-expression
3 **Use of Time** 1 to 10						
Rating number				> Range: 7-10		
Words Top 3 to 5			>	> Perfect timing, fast enough, but not a rush		
4 **Do For – Do To** 1 to 10						
Rating number			7			
Words Top 3 to 5			> Sales assistant was polite and charming, bit not necessary (not in a bad way) Smart "website structure" and helpful filter	>		
5 **Quotes** "........."	Select exact quotes (use separate notes if needed)	"ChanX or nothing"	"Just the original ChanX page, don´t settle for less" "Even the landing page is my inspiration" "I never want to leave"	> "Seconds. We talk about seconds. Amazing job ChanX" "The checkout could have gone on longer" ChanX"	> "Never without ChanX" "I want that everyone has the chance to experience ChanX"	"I want everyone to know that I am a proud owner of ChanX" "I also recommend you to shop at ChanX"

FIGURE 3.11, 2 OF 3

FIGURE 3.11, 1 OF 3

Interaction Name Interaction number		Discovery 1	Consideration 2	Visit the Shop 3	After Purchase 8	User Experience 9	Advocacy 10
Off Internet	Interaction type	Discover new trends and inspiring styles	The decision immediately goes to ChanX. No decision based on general product category but only on a high brand awareness towards ChanX. Information search about ChanX products. (First brand decision, after that the product overview)	Visit to the ChanX store in Munich, especially kept a whole day free for this visit.	Exit the store and "Goodbye"	The user experience and the product is evaluated by the customer with the service	Customer has the opportunity to become a brand ambassador and share experiences
	Interaction description	Inspiration and discovery: People on the street, Shopwindows	Active exchange and high emotional involvement: ChanX store, Friends	Security at the beginning to door and sales assistant is waiting directly in the store	Champagne is offered lost, Sales assistant escorts to door and says goodbye, official conclusion of the in-store experience	The purchase and user experience is described to friends and family, product tell about product and experience	Proudly carry the product in public and tell about product and experience
On Internet	Interaction type	Discover the new trends and styles worldwide	The decision immediately goes to ChanX. No decision based on general product category but only on a high brand awareness towards ChanX. Information search about ChanX products. (First brand decision, after that the product overview)	Opens the own website of Chapel from the laptop at home	Purchase is confirmed, E-Mail is sent with the confirmation and details of delivery	The user experience with the service and the product is evaluated by the customer	Customer has the opportunity to become a brand ambassador and share experiences
	Interaction description	Inspiration and discovery: Social media (Snapchat + Instagram + TikTok + Twitter, Brand communities, Blogs, Online magazines (Vogue)	Active exchange and high emotional involvement: Marketplace, Brand community, Social Media, Specific Apps, Blogs, Magazine, ChanX website	Direct input of Chapel in the "search bar".	Personalized email, click on the invoice and live tracking	The purchase and user experience is shared online with acquaintances, friends and family, including photos / videos of the product. Social media includes Snapchat + Instagram + TikTok + Twitter.	Report the experience via texting and on the Internet and share content (including videos and photos) about the product. Social media includes Snapchat + Instagram + TikTok + Twitter.

Interaction Name / Interaction number		Discovery	Consideration	Visit the Shop	After Purchase	User Experience	Advocacy
		1	2	3	8	9	10
6 Evaluators estimate of likelihood the interaction will create a customer Advocate	Rating number (1=not likely; 10=Very likely)	3	10	10	9	8	9
	Why?	A lot of inspiration and styles, not only ChanX	Talk about the products and ChanX. Inspire other people	Unique experience, "once in a lifetime"-experience, Service	> Happy and proud about the product, "Inspire" other, high emotional involvement	Family and friends can see the emotional value for the customer	WOM, interesting = unique experience, many people are interest in the story
7 Your recommendation: Fix to as is / Improve / Innovate		X	X	X	X	X	X
7a Decision description — Explain why. What is the benefit of decision?		High brand awareness. ChanX is one of the most popular brands, known for iconic pieces and extravagant fashion shows	Most people think directly of ChanX when they think of luxury. Most consumers want to buy directly from ChanX. For this reason, the presence at consideration must continue to be so successful.	The store experience is the USP of the brand and is very relevant. In addition, a high customer experience is to be enjoyed during the store visit.	> Online, the process was fast, but it could still be added an exclusive service. For this reason, you would even create a differentiation online, to ensure this.	Consumers are proud and satisfied consumers. However, we must continue voluntarily promote the brand. ChanX must continue to promote exclusive service, best quality and innovation.	ChanX has a loyal customer base who voluntarily promote the brand. For this reason, continue to promote exclusive service, best quality and innovation.
7b "How" description — Brief description of how to fix, improve, innovate the interaction		Focus must continue to increase brand awareness also continue to prove itself as top of mind.	ChanX must continue to ensure success and continue to prove itself as top of mind.	Continue to intensify the training of sales personnel and continue to successfully provide exclusive additional services.	> Through a selection of small samples that the customer is allowed to choose online, ChanX can also offer an excellent experience online. These samples can encourage further purchases.	Through a small QR code that can be sent online via mail or given offline through a nice card, customers can give their feedback. For this reason, the relationship can be strengthened. ChanX achieves direct feedback and consumers have a strong sense of a brand community.	By constantly analyzing how to make consumers even happier could maintain the standard.

FIGURE 3.11, 3 OF 3

FIGURE 3.11 Interactions evaluated with a customer interaction evaluation template tool now populated by the findings, used in the analysis and with recommendations in brief (as shown). Including important customer quotes; likelihood of the present interaction state to create advocacy and why; recommendations to fix, improve or innovate the interaction; decision description brief of why and how from written report.

9) Select insights from the analysis section. Insights are the discoveries made from the findings and analysis of your customer interviews that will help you make effective decisions to fix, improve or innovate a customer experience interaction or the entire experience. Insights may give ideas about strategies, tactics and operations about customer experience and the business. Specific insights are selected from the analysis and copied into the insights section. A thorough and well-thought-out analysis, with its numbers and words from customers, combined with knowledge of the business and objectives (for this example, the two objectives in our small-scale, non-automated introduction overview stated earlier), will give focus to and important rationales for next steps. The insights are chosen based on how likely they are to help fix, improve or innovate a customer interaction. Or do the same for a strategy, tactic or operation related to the customer experience. In selecting insights, be sure to bring along the important numbers and words upon which they are based to keep the "why" part strong for the next step.

10) Recommendations. Make recommendations based on specific insights and the CX project objectives for each of the interactions and implications for the overall strategy. Recommendations to keep as-is, fix, improve or innovate and the reasons why. Describe in detail what the business and customer can expect after the experience improvement or innovation is made. Do the same for strategy, tactic or operational insights. Again, be sure to include the numbers and important words from the

customer input. Also, include in the recommendations the expected impact on internal measures, those that customers care about and important qualitative aspects of the experience. For example, what positive differences are expected in the CXI for the CX4 or PX5?

> **Time to insights—the measure of how long it takes for an organization to develop insights from its customer experience intelligence is very important now. It will be an increasingly critical success factor for future competitiveness, profitable market entry and survivability. The same is true for reducing time to decision making from those insights.**

The importance of time to insights

Time to insights—the measure of how long it takes for an organization to develop insights from its customer experience inputs—is very important now and will be a critical success factor for future competitiveness, profitable market entry and survivability. The same is true for time from insights to decision-making and time from decision-making to customer experience effectiveness and the bottom line—all of which makes what is coming next, advanced CXI, very important.

Advanced CXI for next-generation CX

The coming advancement of customer experience intelligence is characterized by multiple inputs, partial to near-fully automated analysis and real-time insights. It is made possible by a subset of customer experience leaders, improvements in technology and an increasingly human-centric focus on product and service development.

% of Portfolio Output

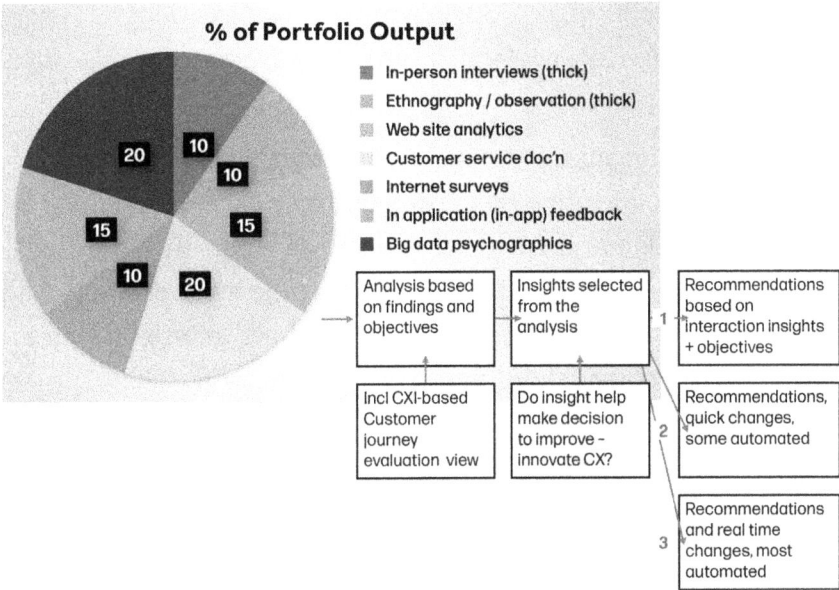

- In-person interviews (thick)
- Ethnography / observation (thick)
- Web site analytics
- Customer service doc'n
- Internet surveys
- In application (in-app) feedback
- Big data psychographics

Analysis based on findings and objectives	Insights selected from the analysis	1 — Recommendations based on interaction insights + objectives
Incl CXI-based Customer journey evaluation view	Do insight help make decision to improve - innovate CX?	2 — Recommendations, quick changes, some automated
		3 — Recommendations and real time changes, most automated

FIGURE 3.12 An example of the sources of information inputs that can be included in the customer experience intelligence portfolio with the addition of varying blends of human and automated involvement and quicker CXI-based interactions changes.

Transformation to real-time business intelligence

The next-generation customer experience intelligence will see a transformation from static or occasional intelligence to dynamic customer experience inputs to insights to actions.

Those organizations with high-frequency or continuous, real-time experience intelligence inputs and quick transformation of the inputs into insights, recommendations and actions will create customer experience leadership for their businesses.

Some organizations are there now. They represent the leading edge of customer experience intelligence of the future by combining big data, internal sales data and customer-specific information anchored by thick data. Those inputs are transformed in a timely way into customer experience improvements and innovation. Here are some examples of companies with next-generation customer experience intelligence: USAA, Workday, Netflix, Google, Apple, Chick-fil-A, ServiceNow, Intuit (TurboTax), Nordstrom, Ally Bank and Newegg.

What these companies have in common is a culture of researching, perfecting and nurturing the customer experience. Where they diverge is in the kinds of customer experience inputs they use, qualitative versus quantitative, how they anchor the input portfolio with thick data and then how they transform inputs to insights and insights to recommendations and actions. Some of the "how" part is proprietary to each organization.

The businesses also share a commitment and an urgency to improve and innovate with dynamic customer experience intelligence. These organizations also use CXI for developing experimental interactions and new customer journeys.

Many of these leaders have their inputs and processes for insights and actions so well-tuned and well-timed that they have been able to go beyond persona profiles to innovate customer experience at the individual level. This type of intelligence can also be predictive of the individual. It can be inspirational, serving as a rich source of knowledge for innovating messages, products and services that will please the individual with an experience in unexpected ways. A welcome surprise!

Inside organizations using advanced CXI are people looking carefully at many types of journeys—customer journeys, support journeys, customer service journeys and user experience journeys. And there are many companies that, in their spacious offices and studios, have people wheeling around massive pieces of plywood in landscape orientation covered with the customer journey steps for their part of the business. One of the authors (Jeof) knows this well after almost being clipped by a product manager wheeling such a board in a rush to an important meeting about next-generation customer experience of a well-regarded software product. It was both frightening and educational at the same time.

Whether in digital or analog form, each interaction of a customer journey is accompanied by qualitative and quantitative information and insights. In several cases, each interaction is also augmented by information about specific personas, including the probability that the persona would proceed to the next interaction in the customer journey as well as the likelihood they would advocate based on that interaction.

Whether you are just beginning to transition data and words into insights or are a company that represents the customer experience intelligence of the future, the important thing is that you are doing it and it is effective for your business and for your customers.

If you want to bring the advantages of competing with customer experience to your organization, think about where you are with CXI now and then carefully and thoughtfully develop the definition of next-generation CXI. Whether it's a two-input method to test or you have the good problem of transitioning a well-running customer experience intelligence method from a low-frequency decision-making contributor to a more dynamic and consistent one, it's important that the quality of your CXI is in the hands of people who genuinely care about experience people have with your business.

Next-Gen Economics is Behavioral Economics for Customer Experience

A more realistic predictor of what people are likely to do—an introduction

"The person who controls the options that are presented to us controls our behavior and our decisions. We may think that we have free will but contextual cues in the design are responsible for a big part of our behavior."

—Dr. Liraz Margalit, Ph.D., a social psychologist specializing in behavioral design and decision-making

CHAPTER 4 Overview

Richard Thaler and the Nobel Prize for Economics - Behavioral economics	Where did the new economics come from?	New economic principles lead to customer experience and business advantages	Using next-generation economics to help achieve next gen CX leadership	Additional resources to consider for you and next-generation CX economics

On October 9, 2017, Richard Thaler, professor of behavioral science and economics at the University of Chicago, was awarded the Nobel Prize for Economics. This recognition was for his important role as one of the founders of the next generation of economics. Thaler is a person with mild dyslexia, a habit of daydreaming and a dislike for tedious work.[47] Yet he, along with several other people, developed a new and more effective economics called behavioral economics.

Thaler proved to many people, including other economists and astute businesspeople, the importance of including human behavior to make more accurate, prescriptive and predictive economic decisions.

This thinking has had a positive impact on almost all decisions related to economics and people, including those involving businesses, customer and user experiences.

Behavioral Economics for Customer Experience:
A more realistic view of what people will do or may do.
Behavioral economics differs from tradition economics by including insights from human behavior.

Considers that most people make systemic mistakes
in decision making.

Includes the context that people make decisions within
as a major influence on the choices people make.

FIGURE 4.1 Three of many principles likely to improve monetary, people and experience decisions.

Until Thaler showed that people's behavior can be complex and irrational, many important economic decisions assumed that people are essentially rational and make monetary decisions specifically to optimize their well-being. This idea, or simplification, allowed for the creation of economic models and decisions separated from human behavior. New economics places priority on understanding the judgments and choices we make.[48, 49]

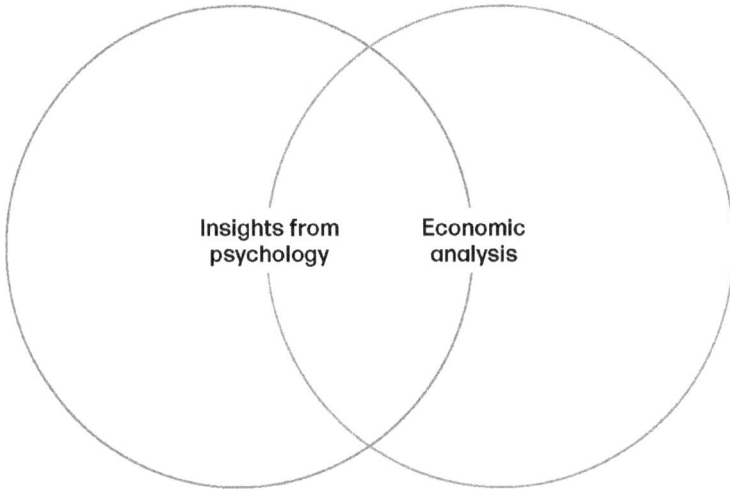

FIGURE 4.2 Insights and actions are determined from behavior and economics.

Where did the new economics come from?

Behavioral economics is built on a foundation of over 40 years of testing in the lab and in the real world. It will be vital to apply it for a better understanding of next-generation customers and their decisions.

While many consider 18th-century Scottish economist Adam Smith to be the father of economics, Smith was also a keen observer of human behavior, something that became dissociated from economics in later years. He recognized that people are often overconfident in their own abilities. They are more afraid of losing than they are eager to win. They are more likely to pursue short-term rather than long-term benefits. These ideas (overconfidence, loss aversion and self-control) are foundational concepts in behavioral economics.[50]

What we know today as behavioral economics was begun by Israeli psychologists Amos Tversky and Daniel Kahneman, who focused their work on people, economics, uncertainty and risk. In the 1970s and 1980s, Tversky and Kahneman identified several consistent biases in the way people make judgments.[51]

One of those biases is that people want to avoid loss. This has an impact on the choices we make, including economic ones. Tversky and Kahneman's research on human behavior illustrates how people are irrational when it comes to decisions about money. Take for instance their "prospect theory." They demonstrated how framing and loss aversion influence the economic choices.

Framed choices #1   **Framed choices #2**

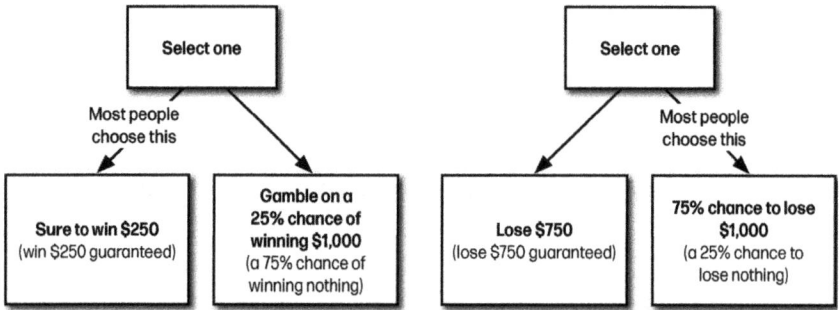

FIGURE 4.3 Tversky and Kahneman proved that framing and loss aversion influence choices people make.

For example, if presented with an opportunity to win $250 guaranteed or gamble on a 25% chance of winning $1,000 and a 75% chance of winning nothing, most people will choose the sure win. But if presented with the chance to lose $750 guaranteed or a 75% chance to lose $1,000 and a 25% chance to lose nothing, most people will risk losing $1,000, hoping for the slim chance that they will lose nothing at all. People are more willing to take risk if it means avoiding a $1,000 loss versus obtaining a $1,000 win.[52]

The degree to which people's aversion to loss may result in irrational choices is an important example of why economics and psychology needed to be connected, just as insights about irrationality also need to be included in decisions about customer experience.

At a high level, behavioral economics differs from traditional economics in that:

1) It takes into consideration that people have limited and variable rationality.

2) People have social and other preferences that impact their behavior and decisions affecting economics.

3) People have limited self-control.

In the 1980s, Thaler began to build on the work of Tversky and Kahneman, closely collaborating with them. He puts the new economics in context this way: "It has never been my point to say that there is something wrong with people. We are all human beings—homo sapiens. The problem is with the model being used by economists, a model that replaces homo sapiens with a fictional creature called homo economicus, which I like to call an Econ for short."[53]

Go beyond success to being significant

Early in his book "Misbehaving," Thaler indicates that historically people are not good at making successful choices for themselves, whether it is buying groceries, picking a career or selecting a spouse.[54] This is an opportunity for customer experience makers to help people make better personal and business selection decisions. In doing so, a company can increase the likelihood of transitioning from being a successful business to the higher order of being a significant business to the customer, their industry and the economy.

Behavioral economics is to conventional economics what human-centered design is to conventional design. In both cases, the generation of economic information and website design decisions (for instance) result from a solid connection to people's behavior. This helps to create more effective customer experiences and business decisions. Behavioral economics has been proven in the real world through a variety of methods and conditions, creating a new, more effective kind of economic intelligence. In turn, this can create a new, more effective contribution to customer experience intelligence.[55]

The topic of behavioral economics is vast and hopefully after reading this chapter you will want to explore more about it and its practical and innovative benefits for customer experience and business development.

FIGURE 4.4 Customer and user experience decisions include behavior and economics together.

New economic principles lead to new customer experience and business advantages

Here are some examples of behavioral economics principles, customer experience best practices and what they can mean for customer and user experiences. Applying these with your own customer experience intelligence (CXI) can lead to new and more interconnected customer experiences, ones likely to increase interaction(s), desirability, customer advocacy and profitability. The 12 examples below are numbered for reference but not in any special order.

1. The human experience comes before the economic outcome

In many markets there are important differences in how each buyer accounts for and experiences affordability. This will impact whether the customer experience is engaging or not. And whether the economic outcome of the experience will be positive or not. In their book "Nudge: Improving Decisions About Health, Wealth, and Happiness," Richard Thaler and Cass Sunstein underscore that people make decisions with "consistent irrationality."

Consistent irrationality and differences in what each person determines is affordable are among the many reasons why understanding customers more deeply and contextually is part of developing a sustainable and valuable customer experience.

Even the most focused business-to-business buyer, seemingly rational, is a person having a human experience. The possibility of irrationality creeping in or dominating a person's decision-making experience exists. This makes understanding how people will behave in response to your economic offer very important if you want to avoid negative outcomes. Testing how people will react to your offer and the interactions related to it, before you scale-up your decisions, can reduce guesswork and minimize risk for you and the customer. It can also guide in making changes to increase advocacy. See Chapters 3 and 6, and the resources at the end of this chapter for ideas about methods of testing.

2. Don't separate people from your economic decisions
Whether it's a price change, a new way of charging people for products or services or any other alteration that may impact customer value for money or time, include customers, guests or patients in the development process before final decisions are made. One way of doing this is to test the outcomes of your economic offers with a subset of representative customers (users and influencers too) before your proposed choices impact most or all customers.

3. I'll do it myself if it saves me time
Typically, people do not want businesses to offload miscellaneous tasks to them, unless it provides them with a time saving and/or

convenience. For instance, people do not want to take on the job of administrator of their bank accounts. Yet they are happy to do administration online if it saves a trip to the bank. At grocery stores, customers are willing to do self-checkout and bagging if it saves them time. Providing self-service options like these that offer time savings or other efficiency improvements for customers is likely to work in the long term.

One of the authors (Jeof) once worked in the business data services division of a large telecom company. The public use of the Internet was still relatively new but rapidly gaining popularity as a business-to-business technology. Leadership made a purely economic decision to replace interactions with direct sales people and data networking experts with a self-service website for many of our top customers. The thinking was that it would save the company time and money. It would also save the customer time.

It was pointed out that we did not have any information or data measuring the value these customers put on their relationship with their direct salesperson and data networking expert. We didn't ask any of them. Would customers appreciate the autonomy or be insulted that the company saw no value in having a human relationship with them? We had no way to know. But the amount of money the company would save was far too attractive and the decision was made.

Within the next year or so many of these customers left and took their data services and important revenue streams to our competitors. The company suffered significant monetary and goodwill losses. While forcing these important buyers into self-service made in-year earnings look better, the net savings beyond this was very small. This excludes the unmeasured impact of un-advocacy from our customers.

These former customers were not shy about letting us know that it was our knowledgeable direct sales representatives and the complex problem-solving of our data networking experts that they valued most in their relationship with us.

The company eventually recognized the decision was a mistake and changed course to correct it. It took 18 to 24 months to bring some of the customers back on board to regain lost revenues. The company culture had rejected the idea of checking with customers about how the impacts of what was viewed as an internal economic decision would affect them.

4. Say-do: Understanding the difference is critical

What people say they will do and what they will actually do are not necessarily the same. The "say" may be rational, yet the "do" could be quite different and less rational. This say-do gap emphasizes the importance of including thick data in your customer experience intelligence. Thick data is gathered by directly interviewing people or by blending into or joining a group of people (a practice called ethnography, borrowed from sociology) to observe their behavior. This is a very direct way of answering specific questions and gaining quality insights about people while in context of their environment (see Chapter 3 for more about this). Including thick data with other less direct data methods will help you better understand if say-do gaps exist, how far apart they are and if irrationality is present.

The goal of blending into or joining a group of people is to not be disruptive, so as to learn in a close-up, natural way. It is done ethically and either with specific questions in mind or with the idea of learning by observing. Even with the idea of learning by observing it takes a disciplined process to understand people and then apply the learnings for economic and customer experience decisions.

Working with many companies, we have seen that including results from in-person interviewing and ethnographic observation (directly in-person or using other face-to-face tools like Zoom or FaceTime) with hard data such as website analytics, psychographics or big data increases our understanding about the size of say-do gaps.

For example, uncovering discrepancies between the number of times a customer says they did something during a website interaction and what they actually did can be invaluable. You also get additional human context important for your decisions to improve the experience and business performance of that interaction.

Intuit, Tesla, Stitch Fix[56] and ServiceNow are some of the more well-known customer and user experience leaders that utilize ethnography. Yet the accessibility and advantages of ethnography are available to early-stage and small organizations too. Ethnography can be learned by taking a course or getting mentored by an experienced ethnographer. Other ways include hiring an expert to train your people or do a project for you.

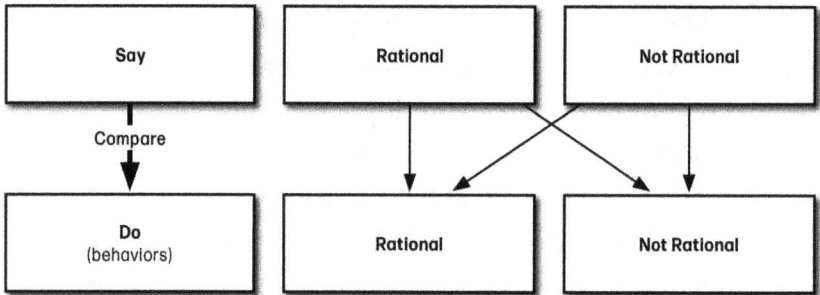

FIGURE 4.5 Say-do comparison boxes.

The understanding of the relationship, or lack of it, between what people say and what they do with observation and qualitative and quantitative information is critical in developing customer and user experiences people will want to repeat and recommend to others.

5. Other people's money may not easily be yours

Convincing people to change their spending plans or habits in your favor may not be easy. Yet understanding how flexible those spending plans or habits are, and how people think about affordability, can help you create customer and user experiences that can convince people to purchase your offer. Using customer experience intelligence with behavioral economics principles to better understand spending flexibility will help you get there.

Conventional economics assumes money is fungible, readily changeable to adapt to new situations, like spending on a new product, service or experience. Thaler proved that this is not the case. Differences in individual "mental accounting" related to affordability and the perceived flexibility of reassigning the purposes of their money can vary vastly.[57] For instance, if money is saved for a vacation, its likelihood of being reassigned to be spent on something else could be reduced if the mental accounting includes a lot of "it depends" variables specific to the individual. It may include the collective mental accounting of other family members or friends.

Is there such thing as extra money? When talking with friends and family about what purchases we would like to make or vacations we would like to take, there are many different opinions about what affordable means.

Consider paying for streaming channels or purchasing an electric vehicle. In our experience, the context of the discussion typically stretches well beyond money. Logic, emotion, environmental concerns and many other topics come up.

Understanding the different mental accounting models and priorities of people you want as customers, guests or patients is essential for giving them valuable and desirable experiences.

Use that understanding to design important aspects of their interactions with your company so that you use their time well, make each interaction valuable and aim to create positive emotions during the experience. Their view of the experience after they compare it with their thoughts about its affordability will have a significant impact on them recommending the experience to others.

6. Understand people's perception of cost compared with total cost

It is important to understand your customer's total cost of purchasing your offer. Then be sure your customer understands what their total cost of buying your offer is. Do they have a perception of total cost much different than real total cost? If the difference is large or has the potential to create disappointment or shock, you could be in trouble. Word of mouth and social media may work against you and your brand.

Certainly, the total cost of products and services can go beyond the money that is paid for them. There can be indirect yet related costs such as travel, shipping or insurance. There may be a cost in time, risk, emotion, environmental impact or other factors very dear to customers.

The importance of customer awareness of total cost before purchasing will increase as more members of the next generation, Gen Z, become your customers and influencers of others. Most Gen Zs are less accepting of surprises about actual cost of products, services and experiences compared to prior generations. Helping them avoid a shock based on total cost will pave the way for doing business with other next-generation customers. (See Chapter 2)

7. How do your customers handle and keep money?

To develop a clear picture of household economics, Thaler highlights the value of understanding how people hold their money.[58] How do they handle it? How do they keep it? Do they save? Do they invest? Are your customers or potential customers living paycheck to paycheck? Do they carry very little cash but own a portfolio of mutual funds, stocks or other investments?

These insights shed light on their priorities, their strategic and tactical orientation and how they value time. This understanding, typically sought-after by financial advisers, is very helpful to those creating and delivering customer and user experience strategies and interactions (for more, see Chapter 6). Businesses can create their own views about how people hold their money from the analysis and insights of their CXI portfolios. Alternatively, engage a qualified outside insights provider such as Claritas or other psychographics/lifestyle research companies.

8. How do pleasing customer interactions measure up to ones that disappoint?

How many chances do you get to please a customer before they move to a competitor, a substitute or, worse, actively un-recommend you? How many customer interactions do you have to delight them before they will advocate for you?

Even if we answer the above questions, it still leaves us wanting to know how to compare the impact of pleasing customer interactions versus disappointing ones. Thaler quantified people's loss aversion and determined that, "Losses hurt about twice as much as gains make us feel good."[59] Thus, to create active advocacy, customer experience interactions need to make customers feel good at a 3-to-1 ratio or more.

> **Interactions need to make customers feel good at a 3 to 1 ratio or more**

Finding out what these ratios are for your customers (or guests or patients) is critical for improving experiences for them—and for increasing advocacy and realizing the benefits of customer experience leadership.

9. Build online decision-making choices that are desirable, rewarding and ethical

In the online realm, the default choices and interactions customer experience makers create for users are purposely developed to be desirable and rewarding for people and profitable for the company.

This is what "Nudge" authors Sunstein and Thaler call choice architecture—the environment in which we make decisions.

Dr. Liraz Margalit, Ph.D., a social psychologist specializing in behavioral design and decision-making, shares this perspective: "The person who controls the options that are presented to us controls our behavior and our decisions. We may think that we have free will but contextual cues in the design are responsible for a big part of our behavior. It's hard to underestimate the great power of design, although we hardly pay attention, but that is the brilliance of this." The options and defaults presented online to customers are made with software code, graphics, data and text. They influence the decision to stay and make purchases or leave, to recommend or not recommend.

Customer and user experience leaders test the choices and default settings while they are being developed. They do testing with the specific types of customers and users under varying conditions. This fine-tuning results in online interactions that are beneficial to users and to the business.

This is part of why careful development and testing of the choices and default settings offered online is a critical part of the success of Intuit, ServiceNow, Netflix, Amazon, USAA and Airbnb.[60]

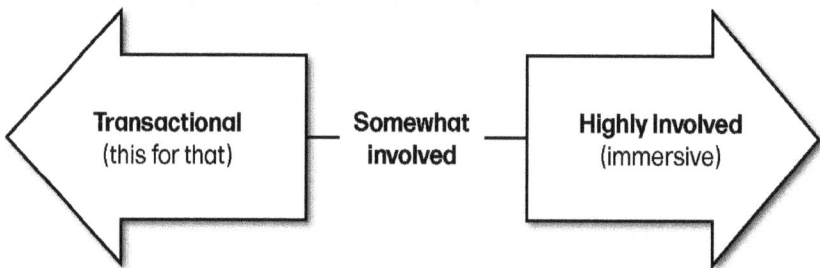

Transactional (this for that) — **Somewhat involved** — **Highly Involved** (immersive)

FIGURE 4.6 Transactional to highly involved customer interaction continuum.

10. Some people want a quick transaction. Others want high involvement.

Conducting business or receiving a service is generally thought of as a transaction. Some customers desire a very basic, simple transaction. This for that. Other people want an engaging and more involved interaction.

The same person may prefer a simple transaction for one interaction and a much more interconnected or involved one for another. The desire and willingness for involvement is impacted by many factors, including the expectation of what the increased involvement in the interaction will do for them, the involvement in using the customer time, the range of emotions that will be experienced, the complexity of the interaction or entire experience and the expectations of the value of a more involved interaction.

You may want a simple interaction when dropping off clothing at the cleaners but seek a more involved interaction when buying clothing or dining. An office manager may want a transactive experience when reordering supplies online but prefer a more immersive one when viewing new office furniture online and buying it in-person.

Understanding where customers fall on the transactional-to-highly-involved continuum becomes more important in creating online and offline interactions as the number of choices increase.

If a person is extremely transactive, they want speed, efficiency and limited involvement. If they want a highly involved interaction, they're usually willing to spend their time and attention. Think of it as a mini relationship!

The interaction to be created for each of these two types of people is quite different. Understanding this fact is more important with users of digital technology because digital sets people's expectations, whether on the internet or off, for how quickly something should happen. As to answering the question of how different types of people prefer to engage, and whether they want those engagements as quick transactions or more involved interactions, using a carefully selected combination of thick data and other types of data about customers will help to understand and decide which kind of interaction will be effective for each type of customer. See chapters 3 and 6 for more about this.

11. Don't make me think (too much)

Steve Krug's book "Don't Make Me Think" is one of best references and most insightful reads about creating successful internet experiences for real people and it occupies an important place in next-generation economics. It's about the behavioral economics of cognitive loads—as in, don't burden the customer or user with clunky, counterintuitive interfaces or processes. Krug isn't implying that people using a web site or mobile device are foolish or ignorant but rather that they probably have a lot on their mind in addition to trying to interact with your company online. Also, you have to take into account the environment they're in, their priorities, their preferred style of interacting and their familiarity with digital devices.

If an interaction can be lightened for people by reducing its cognitive load and stress, the experience will be enhanced and, typically, made more desirable. That is why leading customer experience makers such as Apple, Square, Intuit, ServiceNow and others put so much up-front effort (in design and testing) into making customer experience interactions as intuitive for people as possible. What one person considers a light and reasonable cognitive load may be an overload for another.

12. Start with the customer experience and work back to the technology

"You've got to start with the customer experience and work backward to the technology. You can't start with the technology then try to figure out where to sell it."[61] While Steve Jobs said this many years ago, it's truer than ever as technology plays a growing role in most people's lives. He was thinking about what people wanted technology to do for them. And how they wanted it to do it. Getting this right is a critical part of effective and profitable experience development.

Combining customer and user insights about behavior, technology and economics for developing experiences for people is a key part of the success of many customer experience (CX) leaders. This will continue to be a decisive advantage for next-generation CX leadership.

Just a sampling

The preceding has been just a sampling of next-generation economics principles relating to customer and user experience. There are many established principles and additional best practices of behavioral economics for you to discover. Each can be very helpful in contributing to your development of economically effective and innovative customer experience strategies, tactics and interactions. Now let's look at a path to consider including them as part of your CXI and decision-making.

Using next-generation economics to achieve customer experience leadership

Begin by developing behavioral economics profiles for prospective and existing customers and users. Select a set of next-generation economics principles. Then gain customer experience intelligence about each principle for specific types of customers and users. Analyze the findings for insights. What does it mean for your experience strategies and interactions for each customer type? Then apply the insights when developing customer and user experience strategies and interactions for each of the customer and user types.

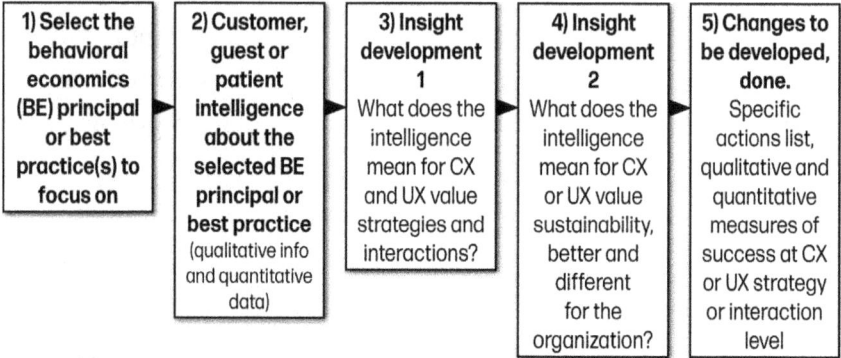

1) Select the behavioral economics (BE) principal or best practice(s) to focus on	2) Customer, guest or patient intelligence about the selected BE principal or best practice (qualitative info and quantitative data)	3) Insight development 1 What does the intelligence mean for CX and UX value strategies and interactions?	4) Insight development 2 What does the intelligence mean for CX or UX value sustainability, better and different for the organization?	5) Changes to be developed, done. Specific actions list, qualitative and quantitative measures of success at CX or UX strategy or interaction level

Manual, automated or hybrid methods to do each step?

Illustration below using the example above: Understand people's perception of cost compared with total cost.

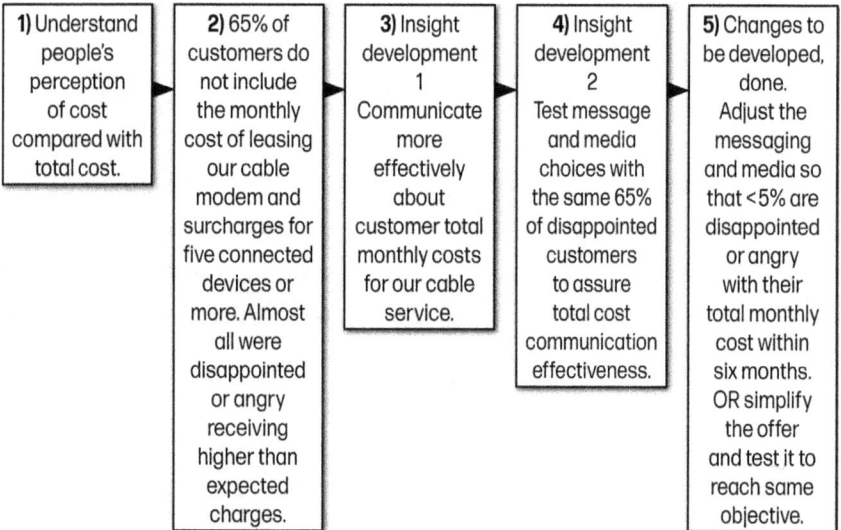

1) Understand people's perception of cost compared with total cost.	2) 65% of customers do not include the monthly cost of leasing our cable modem and surcharges for five connected devices or more. Almost all were disappointed or angry receiving higher than expected charges.	3) Insight development 1 Communicate more effectively about customer total monthly costs for our cable service.	4) Insight development 2 Test message and media choices with the same 65% of disappointed customers to assure total cost communication effectiveness.	5) Changes to be developed, done. Adjust the messaging and media so that <5% are disappointed or angry with their total monthly cost within six months. OR simplify the offer and test it to reach same objective.

FIGURE 4.7 A beginning attempt to apply selected next-generation economics (top) and example (bottom).

You will be more effective if you consistently make behavioral economics part of your CXI portfolio and the resulting insights. If your company keeps and updates personas, add the selected principles and corresponding customer insights as part of the personas.

If your organization's CXI portfolio is updated at a high frequency or in real time and the insights are at the individual customer or user level, integrate the selected principles and corresponding information into your insight development process. (For more about customer experience intelligence see Chapter 3.)

Next, let's discuss two big changes in the new economics compared to the old—the accelerating speed with which new practical economic information is created and the increasing frequency of economic information being used by people in business and everyday life.

Next-generation economics is high-frequency in real time

The COVID-19 pandemic accelerated a trend that had begun in the five or so years before it: the use of high-frequency data in real time. Whether it's daily airport passenger levels or hour-by-hour credit-card spending,[62] this data was being used by governments and large corporations (including Visa and experience makers Square, Apple and Google[63] and innovative small businesses). Consumers were doing likewise, using mobile apps such as Waze or Google Maps to monitor traffic in real-time, GasBuddy to track rising gas prices or getting delivery-time updates from UPS, FedEx and Amazon by e-mail, text or website.

No matter who's accessing the information, each instance changes the expectations of time and what data can do for people who use it. It's also changing our behavior.

There are three major components enabling and accelerating the use of high-frequency data in real-time, according to *The Economist*. First, it relies on data that is plentiful and directly relevant to real-world problems. People want to know what is happening now with their online orders, the traffic jam they are in, the crowd conditions at the airport and the quality of the air they are breathing. "Second, the economists using this data are keener on influencing public policy. More of them do quick-and-dirty research in response to new policies. Academics have flocked to Twitter (now called X) to engage in debate."[64]

Lastly, the new-generation economics is a much more practical, less theoretical third wave of economics. The real-time revolution is attached much more to people's behavior and the data it creates than earlier generations of economics.[65] If this sounds familiar, it should. It's a part of behavioral economics—with an added turbocharge of speed and frequency.

Wanted: Prescriptive and predictive information

Driving the demand for this is the desire for prescriptive information to help inform or fix things now. This is combined with wanting accurate predictions. What is going to happen to me? My family? My wealth? My business? The demand includes being able to determine a time in the future for the arrival of the data. The time intervals of its delivery are set by consumers of economic information and the insights that go with it.

> There is a flywheel effect created when people use economic data at a high frequency in real time or near real time. That usage momentum continues, driving decisions and behavior changes based on the incoming data. This in turn very quickly creates more data.

There is a flywheel effect created when people use economic data at a high frequency in real time or near real time. That usage momentum continues, driving decisions and behavior changes based on the incoming data. This in turn very quickly creates more data.

The new data is almost immediately stored (on servers) ready for use. The momentum of this process was accelerated in the pandemic by scientists, health care professionals, businesses and consumers, who needed faster and more practical data for decision-making. While there is concern about the accuracy at high speed of some of the data, and sharp bumps to be had from it, this is not enough to curb the demand for it. This includes accelerated creation of economics products and services like databases and special comparison indexes for businesses and individuals. These will be provided by data companies and economics services businesses. Business customers and consumers will also be able to create their own.

Behavioral economics at high frequencies in real time will continue to grow as an important part of next-generation customer and user experiences.

All-you-can-eat seats

Selling the worst seats in a large baseball stadium while making fans happy is a very real economic problem to solve. How would you do it? Less-desirable seats may be very far away from the action or have awkward or obstructed viewing angles. Yet simply making them cheap may not ultimately work for the fans who buy them (sure the seats were inexpensive but if you're miserable, it's not worth it) or the teams who sell them.

However, we see new economics at work when we pair or bundle something with these seats that will change people's attitudes and behaviors so they will purchase and enjoy them. An example is the offer of an "all you can eat" deal to the purchasers of these otherwise objectionable seats that gives them unlimited access to select food and beverage items. This promotion has strong appeal to specific customer types who can only attend baseball games on a budget or those who would not attend without some type of deal.

While these offers have been around for years they are still working well at selling some of the worst seats at the stadiums of Major League Baseball's Cincinnati Reds, Pittsburgh Pirates and Texas Rangers. The Rangers all-you-can-eat seat offer is for seats "located in the right field area of the Upper Concourse in Sections 233 through 237. Seats include unlimited grilled chicken sandwiches, hot dogs, nachos, hamburgers, peanuts, popcorn and soft drinks."[66]

Similarly, the Arizona Diamondbacks play at Chase Field where the all-you-can-eat seats include sections 221, 222 and 223 at the ballpark's Diamond Level. Fans can feast on hot dogs, potato chips, peanuts, popcorn, water and soda.[67]

The continued success of these offers is proof of behavioral economics in action. By understanding and catering to the seating and eating desires of a certain segment of baseball fans, stadium operators are selling tickets that might otherwise go unpurchased—which is obviously good for them—while also fostering goodwill by giving fans an inexpensive (and filling!) time at the ballpark.

Additional resources to consider for you and next-generation economics

Acquiring an understanding of customers, users and influencers from a modern economics perspective can help develop desirable and sustainable interconnections with your organization. Doing this is an opportunity to gain a decisive competitive advantage over those unwilling to invest in the work required to learn about and use behavioral economics insights for customer experience leadership.

When behavioral economics becomes a natural part of how you make customer experience decisions and measure them to desired outcomes, you will have taken important steps toward next-generation customer experience leadership! Here are some resource recommendations to help you get there.

Books

- "Misbehaving: The Making of Behavioral Economics," by Richard H. Thaler
- "Nudge," by Richard H. Thaler and Cass R. Sunstein
- "Noise: A Flaw in Human Judgment," by Daniel Kahneman, Olivier Sibony and Cass R. Sunstein

- "The Elements of Choice: Why the Way We Decide Matters," by Eric R. Johnson

Watch or listen to Richard Thaler's Nobel presentation

- Nobel Lecture: Richard Thaler, The Sveriges Riksbank Prize in Economic Sciences, The Nobel Prize
  https://www.youtube.com/watch?v=ej6cygeB2X0 or
  https://youtu.be/ej6cygeB2X0

Join or follow associations/organizations

- Behavioral Scientist is a non-profit digital magazine
  https://behavioralscientist.org/four-roles-for-a-behavioral-scientist-within-your-organization/
- The Journal of Economic Behavior and Organization
  https://www.sciencedirect.com/journal/journal-of-economic-behavior-and-organization/about/aims-and-scope
- The Institute for Behavioral Economics
  https://www.behavioral-economics.org/
- The Society for the Advancement of Behavioral Economics
  https://sabeconomics.org/

Best Practices in Customer Experience Leadership

Foster CX leadership success with examples and experiences from the best

"We see our customers as invited guests to a party and we are the hosts. It's our job every day to make every important aspect of the customer experience a little bit better."

— **Jeff Bezos, founder and CEO, Amazon**

CHAPTER 5 Overview

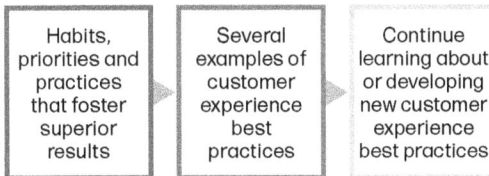

Habits, priorities and practices that foster superior results	Several examples of customer experience best practices	Continue learning about or developing new customer experience best practices

Consider the top 5% of customer experience companies, small and large. In these organizations, there is a culture that fosters leadership habits, priorities and practices. These proven best practices are very effective in attaining superior results—a high number of customer advocates, increased profit margins, low cost of acquiring new customers.

Whether you are a company committed to transitioning to next-generation customer experience leadership or a customer experience leader who wants to maintain or grow your leadership position, the practices discussed in this chapter are indispensable. While new best practices of customer experience leadership are constantly being innovated, the ones we have included here are at the core of CX success for the company and the customer, patient or guest.

Start with one or select several of these best practices. Integrate them into your organization's process of developing strategies and tactics for customer interconnection (see Chapter 6). Make them part of your culture of decision-making for improving and innovating customer interactions.

And before moving on to selected examples of CX best practices below remember that customer experience best practice "number zero" is knowing, applying and benefiting from present-day CX best practices.

1. Business leaders need to commit to customer experience

Being a customer experience leader requires commitment and understanding from the top, whether you are a two-person business or a Fortune 500 company. Customer experience is not a project assigned to a small group of people or a department or division. Valuing customer experience must be a priority for everyone. Whether it's company strategy, tactics or operations, people need to be thinking about the impact of decisions and actions on customer experience.

2. Have a clear definition of customer experience

Having a clear definition of excellence in customer experience for your business and your people is indispensable in reducing any ambiguity around what your organization means by it and setting goals to get there. Be sure that the definition is communicated clearly and that everyone in the company has access to it and understands what it means to the organization and for individuals in it.

The absence of a definition can lead to unfocused discussions and inconsistent service or product development and customer interactions. Often people mistakenly define customer experience as customer service. This is common and creates a myopic view that can result in employees believing they already deliver great customer experiences. Of course, customer service is extremely important but it is only a piece of the total or end-to-end customer experience.

A while back, one of the authors (Jeof) had the opportunity to ask over 600 people at an SDL Innovate conference, hosted by information management solutions provider SDL, "How many of you work at a company that has an official customer experience definition?" Less than 10 people raised a hand.

This response is typical. If you are a company seriously eying a customer leadership position so you can be better and different for your customers and more profitable and longer lasting than the competition, you need a definition of customer experience that is consistent and understood across your organization.

Below is our definition, based on our research, including many interviews with people at companies delivering world-class customer experiences and their customers. It applies to all types of business—business-to-business, business-to-consumer and hybrids. Of course, the definition should be customized to your organization but start with this overall core definition.

Customer Experience (CX) Defined by the Experience Makers
The feelings, thoughts, beliefs and memories people have about all their interactions *with* or *about* a company's messages, people, processes and technologies, products or services. (The customer experience continuum is an organizations people, processes and technologies, products or services.) *continues* ›

When does the experience start?
- From the time a person discovers the company.
- Then when they become a customer and on to being an advocate.

The User Experience (UX) is included in the customer experience. There are usually two kinds:
- A person's experience directly interacting with a company's products or services
- Interacting with an organization's web site, mobile app, digital kiosk or other devices.

Customer experience (CX) defined by leading customer experience makers:

One of the important details in the definition above is the phrase "or about" as it's a good reminder of the importance and influence of indirect customer experiences such as hearing about the company via word of mouth or reading social media posts about it.

3. Commit to customer experience for the long-term

Since Amazon's beginning in 1994, its Founder and CEO Jeff Bezos has never kept it a secret that "Our goal is to be Earth's most customer-centric company." Amazon's three key strategies to build a great customer experience are:

1) Sacrifice short-term gains for long-term value

2) Focus on the customer

3) Continuous innovation[68]

Starbucks Founder and CEO Howard Schultz's customer experience strategy has been "to be a customer's 'favorite third place' after home and work."[69] This has been so since the mid-1980s.

For Amazon and Starbucks, these are not taglines, internal programs or external campaigns. They summarize the culture and goals of these leaders and their companies. They are commitments.

4. Create customer experience buyer personas

A persona, created by gathering and analyzing customer experience intelligence, represents a group of customers who have similar characteristics. The personas are wide and deep profiles and help you create experiences tailored to real people, increasing the chances they will make you their go-to company.

At a minimum, a persona is presented in a one-to-two-page document containing specific customer attributes that helps each person in the company to get to know the customer. Attributes may include how they use the internet, what their preferred devices are or what their buying process is. You may want to include photos—to help everyone remember this is about real people, not just data.

There is no correct number of customer types or personas. The number is whatever you need to be effective at determining your customer experience. And don't just focus on those who buy; remember that the users of your products or services may not always be the ones who paid for them.

Many of the best in customer experience—like Apple, Intuit and Mitchell International—build personas with available (secondary) data and qualitative information. Then they interview or observe several people who match each persona to validate and adjust. The personas need to be fine-tuned regularly to keep the company in the lead in customer experience. Top businesses even use personas to define their vision for future customers.

Mitchell International—experts in provisioning technology, connectivity and information solutions to the property and casualty claims and collision repair industries – is exemplary in the development and application of personas for customer and user experience development. The personas are not only available on their company intranet but they have also placed life-sized cardboard versions of personas throughout their offices.

This CX Buyer Persona Intelligence Development Template Tool is recognized by the International Leadership Association.[70] https://ilaglobalnetwork.org/wp-content/uploads/2021/01/2017_Brussels_ProgramBook.pdf

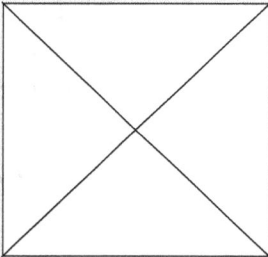

B to C
Persona name here
Text summary here (at a glance)

Photo:

"Personal or Professional Mantra"

Do-Fors
"Best things people, processes, products or services can Do For me"

Opportunities

Challenges

Business or social causes

Notable lifestyle, media, buying traits

Urbanicity   Demographics
Age:
Gender:
Marital Status:
#/Age of Children:
Location:
Occupation:
Job Title:
Annual Income:
Level of Education

Household or Business Technology
          (Below avg to Above avg)
(Postal) Zip Code: (for adding big data)
Car   Lifestyle and media traits
Restaurants
Shops online at
Shops off Internet at
Non-at-work activities
Buying process
Vacation activities
Vacation travel locations
Favorite airlines
Uses social media
Influenced by social media for purchases
Influencer of social media for others purchases
Listens to / music type
Watches types / programs examples
Stays smart (effective) and informed by
Preferred devices to access Internet
Preferred application 1 and for what
Preferred application 2 and for what
Preferred application 3 and for what

FIGURE 5.1 CX Buyer Persona Intelligence Development Template Tool page 1.

This is a selection of proven key elements to consider when selecting from for the business to consumer CX buyer persona intelligence profile.

B to B supplement
Company name here
Industry
Market share
Profit margins compared with industry
Competitors
Leadership
Leadership culture
Metrics of performance (KPIs) internal / external
Economic trends
Formal or informal buying process
Buying process details and requirements

Top industry opportunities

Top company opportunities

Top industry challenges	Uses social media (business specific)
	Influenced by social media for purchases
	Influencer of social media for others purchases
	Listens to podcasts by
	Watches types / programs examples
Top company challenges	Stays smart (effective) and informed by
	Preferred devices to access Internet
	Preferred application 1 and for what
	Preferred application 2 and for what
	Preferred application 3 and for what

FIGURE 5.2 CX Buyer Persona Intelligence Development Template Tool page 2.

This is a collection of proven key elements to consider when selecting from the business-to-business CX buyer persona development template tool. This page (page 2) or set of elements is added to the consumer set above which focuses on the aspects of the person in the business your business will be interacting with. This can vary widely in a set of B2B interactions that, for example, have four important and vastly different persona types over a customer journey having 30 interactions from discovery to advocacy.

5. Know which businesses set your customers' expectations

Your customers likely interact with many businesses. These encounters create a set of expectations. This makes it imperative to have specific insights about which companies are setting the customer experience expectations for your customers at the persona level.

Customer Persona Preferences Along the Customer Experience Continuum

Customer	Messages	People	Processes	Products	Services
Persona 1	Schwan's	Zingerman's Deli	Amazon	Apple iPhone	Nordstom
Persona 2	USAA Insurance	Apple Retail	National Car Rental	Chevy Silverado HD	USAA Insurance
Persona 3	Wawanesa	Cabela's	Hotel Indigo	Intuit QuickBooks	Uber

FIGURE 5.3 Differing persona best experience preferences along the customer experience continuum illustrated across the top row.

In the example in Figure 5.3, we look at three important personas or customer types and which company sets the expectation for each part of the customer experience continuum. For example, we see that Persona 1 loves the in-person experience at Zingerman's Delicatessen in Ann Arbor, Mich. If you go there on a cold, gray day in the middle of winter the line of people waiting to get in could stretch out the door and down the block. It's not just the food, it's the experience they crave, one that is so widely celebrated that the company has published its "Zingerman's Guide to Giving Great Service" (as well as a guide to good eating). While you may not run a deli, that doesn't mean you can't replicate certain aspects of the experience so loved by your customers.

Whether a business is B2B, B2C or both, people do not compare the experiences they have in nice, neat industrial categories the way businesses frequently view themselves and their competition. If a customer loves how they were treated at a Four Seasons resort, they may compare that to their experience at a local medical clinic or retail business. The fact that each is a different type of business/ industry is irrelevant to the customer.

6. Define a concierge version of customer service for your market and implement it

Concierge services originated in France as a Parisian idea associated with the attentive care of people living in higher-end apartment buildings—an elite service experience for a few of the wealthiest residents. The best attributes of traditional high-end concierge, digital concierge and luxury concierge, in whole or part, are now being experienced by a much larger number of people. People new to concierge-level service are getting tastes of it from leading customer service experience companies and innovative online businesses delivering digital concierge services as part of the total customer experiences.

Start-ups and small businesses reach new-to-concierge clients with their websites, internet services listings and social media. Examples include firms like addSpace To Your Life!, who specialize in home organization and image advice; WMSE Elite Concierge Services, for personal concierge; and Essential Concierge, which lists themselves as providing event planning and services and being personal assistants and home organizers. (The do-for for clients on their web site is, "Essential Concierge Helps You to Recharge and Enjoy a Most Extraordinary Life.")

Another aspect of the transformation of customer service to concierge-level service is the employee concierge industry. Notable for their benefits to both employees and employers, employee concierge programs can decrease worry and improve employee engagement, recruitment and retention. Best Upon Request is a business strategically focused on services for all levels and types of employees. Their concierges are "trained to do everything from gas tank fill-ups and grocery shopping to planning your department's next celebration."[71]

Additionally, there are pure "digital concierge" services or websites and mobile apps that save clients time and worry, suggest options and help with decision-making. They are increasing people's accessibility to concierge services and in turn raising expectations for concierge-level customer service across a range of industries.

Want to ride this wave? Be one of the people asking, "What is concierge-level service for my industry?" The people and companies answering that question and acting on it in-market are motivated by differentiation, customer retention, profitability and customer advocacy.

7. Take the jargon out of your internal language to get closer and align with customers

Words are powerful, especially the ones people use every day. One of the best ways to connect with and understand customers and transform the company to one with a focus on customer experience is to leave the jargon behind, including the acronyms, that the company uses internally when writing or speaking about customers or customer-related initiatives. What do you replace this language with? The words your customers use! This not only fosters better understanding but it helps to align employees and processes with customers.

8. Big data: the CX accelerator

Big data is large-volume, high-speed data that is transformed into insights for decisions[72] about customer experience[73]. While the use of the term big data may be overhyped, big data is at its best when used to improve customer experiences in many increments over time. Without this focus, big data can result in an expensive exercise that does not create insights for effectively improving an organization's customer interactions and customer experience strategies.

Big data is so critical that there is a specific title for professionals who specialize in extracting and interpreting data created by people using devices attached to the internet: data scientist. The greatest demand for this role now comes from retailers, matchmaking companies like eHarmony or SilverSingles, banks and heavy equipment manufacturers.[74]

"It's about building a mountain with pebbles," says Jim Manzi, CEO of Applied Predictive Technologies, which develops big data processing software.[75] Companies like Google and Amazon that depend on the internet have kept their customer experiences relevant and valuable with multiple incremental gains based on the stream of intelligence from big data. Netflix has used their accumulated data to enhance subscriber experience almost from the time they were a start-up.

It is not just internet or technology companies that use big data. Coca-Cola, UPS and Big Lots are some of the businesses that make use of big data. Experience-maker Starbucks uses big data to keep their customer experiences valuable and be alerted when to fix, improve or innovate new ones.

9. Getting into the thick of it for insights with context and multiple dimensions with thick data

Thick data is information that comes directly from humans, including interviews and observation (ethnography) with nothing in between. Thick data acts as a focusing lens when thoughtfully combined with big data, internal data and other data not gathered directly from people. Thick data adds important context and multiple dimensions about how people experience interactions. It can help make information that is gathered about people, both qualitative and quantitative, relatable to other humans. Tremendous insights for effective decision-making are to be had by combining information gathered directly and indirectly from people. (For more about this see Chapter 3.)

10. The Amazon Prime lesson

Putting the customer and customer experience at the center of evaluating new ideas and projects is a long-term investment. When Jeff Bezos wrote about the introduction of Amazon Prime, which was very experimental and used money that could have been paid out as profits, he said that, "We expect Amazon Prime to be expensive for Amazon.com in the short term." Prime's do-for of "Amazon Prime takes the effort out of ordering" made its customer experience better and different for Prime members. Bezos's letter followed up with, "We hope to earn even more of your business." Having to wait for profitability seems to agitate some dividend-expecting shareholders[76] but over time, Amazon shareholders have learned where the company's value comes from and that when there is a wait, it is well worth it.

11. Understand customer experience time

The top-performing customer experience companies understand the details of how customers view time and use time.

Hundreds of in-person interviews with people at these firms reveal a striking difference between how they define their biggest competitor. Instead of referring to another business as their biggest competitor, leading customer experience companies including Amazon, Netflix and Intuit have told us that their ultimate competition is for the customer's time. A business that can know the customer so well that they can get their time will have a very effective advantage over competitors.

You want customers to feel that every experience with your company is time well or usefully spent—so much so that they will want to tell others about it. When working on customer experience intelligence projects we have asked many customers about specific interactions in ways such as: "How did the company use your time when you called them about the specifications and configuration choices for the public address system you were buying for your business? Please rate the company's use of your time on a scale of 1 to 10, 1 being my time was not well-used and 10 being my time was well-used. And please tell us why you chose that rating."

12. Learn to pivot

Amazon encourages learning from mistakes. They will study what went wrong, look at the data and review the thinking that made the initiative sound like a good idea in the first place. Then they will try to pivot the good parts to perhaps a different customer or different pricing that will better allow them to succeed.

If there is nowhere in the company to pivot, at least they have learned from it, which may prevent future failures. This is part of the Amazon culture of innovation: let people try well thought-out, strategically sound ideas without the fear of failure.

13. Compete by customer experience opportunity

When Apple entered the smartphone market in 2007, the incumbent companies did not take them seriously. Inside some of those companies, there was even laughter and a dismissive attitude. This included companies that were eventually forced out of their smartphone market leadership position including Palm, BlackBerry and Nokia. What was common to all of them was the belief that their leadership position could not be challenged and that Apple's inexperience in their industry would protect them. In retrospect these companies were more interested in their technologies and products than in customers and what they wanted their smartphones to do for them.

About 10 years later, Amazon looked very carefully at the grocery distribution market. They found that the two least-changed and most off-putting interactions for customers were standing in the checkout line and the checkout process itself. This was seen as an opportunity to design a new customer experience for a decisive advantage. This was the beginning of Amazon Go. Technology was developed for a small number of experimental grocery stores where customers can walk in, quickly scan an item and leave the store, effectively eliminating the onerous checkout lines and checkout process. Then Amazon acquired Whole Foods, the high-end, boutique-style grocery chain with large stores. It has been anticipated that Amazon Go technology will be installed to improve the Whole Foods shopping experience at all their 500-plus locations. As of this writing a new, more precise version of Amazon Go named Just Walk Out has been installed for testing at the Whole Foods Market in Washington, D.C.'s Glover Park neighborhood.[77]

> **Eliminating the lines for check out and the check out process so unloved by customers**

Amazon's first messaging to potential customers was, "No lines, no checkout." Not just a tagline but a customer experience do-for. A promise that is well-delivered, as the concept, technology and design of the customer experience was developed with customer participation.

Meanwhile, the reaction of the traditional grocery store industry has been split. And some Whole Foods customers complain that Amazon does not know how to manage grocery inventory and supply chains. If Amazon's history of creating or entering new markets is a predictor (phones, e-readers and physical distribution as examples), the company will overcome these challenges and will continue to innovate the customer experience.

Since the in-store process of customers waiting in line and going through checkout is a major weakness for most retail industries, Amazon has considered licensing its Go technology, or some versions of it, to other companies.[78]

14. Blend the internet and off-internet customer experience to make sense and help customers

A best practice of experience-maker companies such as Intuit, Uber and REI is to blend the digital and physical customer experiences to assure the combination makes sense to customers. Based on customer experience intelligence, leading companies understand how and when people use the internet. One important overarching finding is that many customers integrate use of the internet with non-internet activities.

While this may sound obvious, there are many companies that have stores or offices and websites and keep the website business separate. It may be how the business started or how it is operated but most customers do not separate the two. They typically use both. They may do so at the same time and expect that the physical and internet parts of the business will complement each other and be helpful to them.

Developing customer and user experiences that are consistent with each other on and off the internet is not only more likely to please customers but also more likely to create customer advocates. Advocates that have adopted the company's web site or mobile app as part of their everyday professional or personal life.

15. Create and deliver a customer experience ecosystem

If you have a successful product or service and your customer experience is creating customer advocacy, you now have a great opportunity. It's natural for customers who refer other people to your business or advocate and increase your business through social media to want other products and services from you. You can maximize the benefit of this situation by creating a customer experience ecosystem made up of products or services that they would naturally adopt for their own.

Apple, USAA, Harley-Davidson and Ally Bank are all experience makers, offering a portfolio of products and services that deliver a customer experience, building off of an original product/service. Some of the offers are logical extensions of existing products and services while others are quite different but have the customer experience unmistakably in common.

USAA sells insurance, banking, real estate, investment products and advice and retirement planning. While all are financial services, they are not necessarily related. What is common is a customer experience that is matched to the lifestyle and life stage of their customers.

Harley-Davidson is legendary for their V-twin-powered motorcycles, which are frequently a canvas for owners to personalize with accessories, modifications and paint schemes. Then there is official Harley-Davidson gear and clothing. Customers want to create their view of the Harley-Davidson lifestyle and the company wants to give them plenty of options in their ecosystem to create it. Few companies are as close to their customers as this firm is and has been since 1903. Their customer experience realm even extends to participating with their customers in motorcycle events such as the famous Sturgis Motorcycle Rally and Daytona Bike Week.

In short, extraordinary customer experiences are hard to copy and they offer tremendous sustainable competitive advantages.

16. Supercharging the customer experience with human-centered design

If you use a computer or a phone, Larry Tesler has made your life easier. Tesler passed away in February 2020[79] and while many of the written tributes to him acknowledged that he was the inventor of the "cut," "copy" and "paste" computer commands as well as "find and replace," there was much more to his innovations. He was clearly one of the founders of modern customer experience and user experience. He worked at Xerox Palo Alto Research Center, also known as PARC, where many of the ideas for computer interconnection and e-mail originated. Steve Jobs hired him as vice president and chief scientist, helping to develop the Lisa and Macintosh. Later he worked with Jeff Bezos in charge of Amazon's online shopping experience.

Above all Tesler cared about people. He had a passion for simplifying technology, always keeping the people who would use it in mind. The New York Times shared this excellent early example of his commitment to human-centered design and development: "His first breakthrough at Xerox PARC came when he took a newly hired secretary, sat her in front of a blank computer monitor and took notes while she described how she would prefer to compose documents with a computer. She proceeded to describe a very simple system that Mr. Tesler then implemented with Mr. Mott." This became the Gypsy program, with the first cut-and-paste functions for moving blocks of text and the ability to select text by dragging the cursor through it while holding down a mouse button. This was just the beginning of multiple consecutive innovations.[80]

Global design company IDEO is a leader in developing products people enjoy using. At the heart of their success is human-centered design. IDEO is a best-practice example of how to make user empathy the focus of product development.

The company states that they believe the key to figuring out what humans really want lies in doing two things: "Observing user behavior: Try to understand people by observing them. For example, if you are designing a vacuum cleaner, watch people vacuum. Putting yourself in the situation of the end-user: IDEO does this to understand what the user experience is really like; to feel what their users feel." The insights gained from this are then used in the development and retesting of products.[81]

The Interaction Design Foundation explains it like this: User-centered design (UCD) is an iterative design process in which designers focus on the users and their needs in each phase of the design process. In UCD, design teams involve users throughout the design process via a variety of research and design techniques, to create highly usable and accessible products for them.

IDEO has a history and focus on positive change by design. Examples include Apple's first mouse and Steelcase's Leap chair. IDEO applies user-centered design to create positive product experiences for clients that have included Coca-Cola, ConAgra Foods, Eli Lilly, Ford and Medtronic.

IDEO defines what finished looks like after implementing user-centered design as: "When you understand the people you're trying to reach and then design from their perspective, not only will you arrive at unexpected answers, but you'll come up with ideas that they'll embrace."

Now think about how effective applying human-centered design principles will be for each part of the experience your customers will have on and off the internet.

There are other experience makers (Tesla, Intuit and Apple) that apply these human-centered design principles to the development of each part of the customer experience continuum: the messaging, training and development of their people; the design and development and testing of processes, technologies, products and services. It is immensely powerful and it supercharges the development of the total customer experience.

17. Assure customer experience and user experience are ready before you launch

Interviewing Larry Tesler for the book "The Customer Experience Revolution" was profoundly insightful for one of the authors (Jeof). One of the many gems Tesler shared was from his time as vice president and chief scientist at Apple Computer working with Steve Jobs: "Whether it was positioning the marketing message, or customer service and support, or upgrades and repairs, Steve Jobs usually said, 'Delay the product so you can fix it.'"[82]

While many believe that Jobs was striving for elusive perfection, Tesler shared that Jobs was instead thinking about the customer and user experience. There was no point of meeting a launch date if pieces of the customer/user experience were not as ready as they could be by delaying things a little while. A great experience means people will remember their first encounter with a new product or service much more deeply and positively than if you met your initial launch date but disappointed them with an unpolished offering, inaccurate marketing messages or shoddy support.

These points are more important today for the same reason that customer experience and user experience are more important than ever. It's not just that the overall quality of customer and user experiences has improved but also the fact that people can share their thoughts and feelings quickly and efficiently with social media. If you launch a disappointing product or service, people may not give you a second chance. Savings on the upfront development of CX and UX could cost dearly by jeopardizing customer advocacy or damaging the brand's reputation.

18. Don't make me think

As we touched on in Chapter 4, an effective and insightful book about creating internet experiences is Steve Krug's "Don't Make Me Think: A Common Sense Approach to Web Usability."[83] While Krug originally aimed his book at website and mobile designers, developers, project managers and marketing professionals, it should be read by everyone in companies where customer experience success depends on people using web sites or mobile devices.

The phrase "don't make me think" is not meant to imply that those using a web site or mobile device are stupid or ignorant. Rather, it's an acknowledgment that the applications are competing with many things: what people have on their minds, their priorities, the environment, the conditions of use and their familiarity with digital devices.

Krug's overriding principle is that "When I look at a web page it should be self-evident. Obvious. Self-explanatory. I should be able to 'get it'—what it is and how to use it—without expending any effort thinking about it."

This is the goal of creating an effective and extraordinary internet user experience and it is a vital part of the overall customer experience. If you are already there, you know what a lift it is to the overall customer view of your company, to repeat sales and to the advocacy you receive.

If your company's web experience could use improvement, start by reading Krug's chapter "How We Really Use the Web." Then do some professionally conducted observation of people using your site. No fair giving them any help. The things you see and hear will give you great insight into adjustments and enhancements. We will let Krug have the last words for this best practice: "Knowing some usability principles will help you see problems yourself and help keep you [or your team] from creating them in the first place."

19. Create out-of-box experiences that inspire customers to recommend you!

The out-of-box experience is what happens to people between the time customers get a sealed container with a product or service part in it and when it's been unwrapped and put into use. How well did the unboxing use the customer's time? What did it do for them or, worse, to them? Was it pleasing? Frustrating?

The main goals of developing an extraordinary out-of-box experience are:

1) To please the customer in the shortest possible time from
   opening the box to the having the product deliver its do-fors.

2) To have the customer advocate for you in person, by word of
   mouth and in social media, either based on out-of-box or the
   entire customer experience.

3) Create an out-of-box customer experience that decreases the
   number of returns that customers send back. A high return
   rate decreases manufacturer and distributor profitability and
   likely will disappoint customers.[84]

Based on conducting hundreds of comparison tests with clients,
customers and while teaching customer experience courses at the
University of California San Diego Extension, there is little doubt
that most out-of-box experiences are not pleasing—offering businesses a tremendous opportunity to create an interaction that moti-
vates customers to advocate for their company, product or service.

Effective out-of-box development goes beyond working with good
packaging designers and ad agencies. A human-centered approach
means creating and testing the out-of-box experience with the customer types or personas who will be opening the packaging and
using the product.

For example, we learned a great deal by conducting out-of-box
tests for a consumer electronics company that was suffering from
millions of dollars in returns of perfectly functional product. We
created several internal teams made up of product managers, packaging engineers, salespeople and additional internal marketing and
engineering professionals. Each team opened boxes of their company's products to see how long it took and what it was like.

Some were shocked that assembly was required because there was no hint of this anywhere. Most had never opened any of their firm's packaging. One team, unboxing a portable heater, smelled an odor like burnt toast when the product was first turned on. While the product team knew this was a normal 30-second burning off of a protective coating on the heating coils, nowhere was it explained to the purchaser. As a result, many purchasers had immediately unplugged the device and returned it, thinking it was defective.

Out-of-the-Box Customer Experience Journey Development and Testing Frame

Date, Company and Product _____

Persona name or attach complete persona description _____

Who is doing journey experience testing?_____

Conditions of use: number of people, time, location, environment, primary language:

	Mapping the Out-of-the-Box Customer Journey					**Effectiveness**	
			Step	# of Attempts		Step or product	Ease U
	Step Description	Time on step	Completed Y/N	to completion	# Errors on step?	abandonment? Y/N	of step ma (Discovery, a 1-10+ 1-
0	Sample step: Unbox	5	Y/N	3	2	N	5
1							
2							
3							
4							
5							

FIGURE 5.4 Upper left of the Out-of-Box Experience Development and Testing template.

Which companies are out-of-box experience leaders?

- Apple's iPhone comes pre-charged and the design is so intuitive most customers have no need for an instruction manual.
- Amazon makes sure that each new Kindle is pre-staged with your account information along with any media selections you already own.
- Lego became the benchmark for out-of-box experiences by understanding its young and frequently complex customer personas. "The aesthetic of illustrated, staged, non-verbal construction is rightly considered a classic in the infographics space."[85]

- Asus has a quick and simple out-of-box experience with one of its complex, high-performance wireless routers. Shortly after power-up the router recognizes all nearby internet-dependent devices, connects to the Asus web site and then the owner's account and with just a few inputs from the customer, configures itself in less than 10 minutes.

These customer advocate-creating, bottom-line-building out-of-box experiences were developed on purpose. They are human-centered, enhance the entire customer ethos and benefit the company and the users of its products.

Want to see more examples? Check out the Interaction Design Association's (IxDA) archive of its Interaction Awards, which recognize "excellence in Interaction Design across domains, channels, environments, and cultures." At http://awards.ixda.org/past-years/ .[86]

There are plenty of opportunities for you to be better and different by testing and developing out-of-box experiences that inspire customers to recommend your products and services!

20. Be an employer that creates employee advocacy

There is a correlation between sustainable customer experience leadership and employee experience leadership. In fact, many of the same firms that rank highly in customer experience indices also place similarly in employee experience indices. These companies include Apple, Google, Kaiser Permanente, Kimpton Hotels, Trader Joe's, Intuit and USAA.[87, 88, 89, 90]

Employee experience (EX) indexes like IBM[91], Jacob Morgan[92] and Forrester Research[93] track, measure and qualify the attributes that make places desirable to work—things like belonging, purpose, achievement, happiness and vigor.

Many factors go into making an organization a great place to work. Based on our experience guiding, training and instructing, team effectiveness is a predictor of a great place to work. And it is also highly correlated to success in improving and innovating customer experience.

From customer-facing employees to those with less-direct impact, all have a part in delivering a great experience—and all are important for team effectiveness. "Over 69% of engaged employees indicate a good understanding of customer needs, compared to just 17% of disengaged employees," according to Qualtrics June 2019 data.

IBM findings on the financial impact of a positive employee experience indicate that organizations scoring in the top 25% of employee experience earn twice the return on sales compared to businesses in the bottom quartile.[94] A company that is a top performer in employee experience is more likely to have a customer experience that is more valuable and more sustainable—yet another reason why creating high levels of employee advocacy is a customer experience best practice.

21. Establish a customer experience advisory board to help you transform into a customer experience leader

Also known as a client advisory board or patient advisory board—and different from a traditional customer advisory board or user group—a customer experience advisory board focuses on the complete customer experience, from discovery to advocacy. It helps the company become customer experience-focused or improve the existing CX focus. At least half of the members should be customer experience experts from outside the company who know CX best practices, are successful CX decision makers and understand the leadership culture of the top customer experience businesses.

The rest of the board is populated by happy and not-so-happy customers who have a vested interest[95] in shaping and improving customer experience. Ideally it also includes people like the new customers you want to have.

The advice that comes from this board will guide the company on important actions such as:

- Selecting a set of reference companies along the customer experience continuum
- Understanding where existing and future customers get their experience expectations
- Assessing how good the present customer experience is
- Determining what the new customer experience should be
- Selecting customer experience metrics and integrating them for performance measurement
- Alerting the company when people's expectations of experience change
- Alerting the company if the existing customer life cycle is losing relevance and value
- Serving as a role model for decision-making and a future center of excellence of customer experience

Here are some guidelines for creating and maintaining a successful board from the experts at CustomerAdvisoryBoard.org:

- Get the right group: Develop an effective plan and communication program to recruit and keep the best board members.
- Have the right conversations: Organize your agenda to make sure you get the most from the limited time you have available.
- Provide enough value: Make sure members receive as much tangible value from their participation as you receive.
- Capture strategic insight: Organize to make sure you can separate the truly important from the merely interesting and useful insights.
- Leverage insight and relationships: Have an effective process in place to leverage what you accomplish with board members across your organization. Track progress.

- Measure impact: Be sure you're getting a real return on the time and resources invested. Have appropriate metrics and an effective measurement system in place.

22. Plan, develop and deliver positive emotion for each interaction in your customer's experience

Regardless of whether it's a consumer or business purchase, emotions are one of the most powerful influencers of customer experiences and drivers of motivating advocacy. The best companies in customer experience know this and work to achieve positive emotional outcomes from every interaction.

One very successful business-to-business software and financial services company, whose name needs to remain confidential for this example, tests and develops their interactions with the goal of having a statistically significant probability of excellent emotional outcomes for each interaction. They have these probabilities for each present interaction and goals for a higher likelihood of positive emotional outcomes for future improved or innovated versions.

Feeling good before, during and after interacting with your company is an important predictor of customer advocacy. While establishing an emotional connection with customers may seem an elusive goal, it's worth striving for as it may be the most critical factor to securing the ultimate bond, the ultimate value, in a business relationship.

For more about the importance of developing and delivering positive emotions see Chapter 3.

23. Never stop learning about or developing new customer experience best practices

It's fitting that the last words on best practices in this chapter are about two of the best practices of all: constantly seeking to understand and apply existing best practices and developing new best practices as part of your culture of customer experience leadership.

For those newly committed to focusing on creating and delivering an outstanding customer experience, there is a wealth of existing information on best practices to select and implement in your journey to becoming a leader. The first groups of best practices you select and implement pertain to the beginning of the process. Then, depending on your organization's results, culture and speed with which you can adopt and enact new best practices, you can select the next set.

Commitment and momentum are needed to create new customer experience best practices.

The constant monitoring of customer interactions and the resulting improvements of those interactions is one of the indicators of a successful transition to being a customer experience leader. It also raises the likelihood that people inside your organization or customers will spark the idea for new customer experience strategies and best practices to test and measure.

For those already in customer experience leadership positions, finding or developing the next generation of best practices is part of what you do every day. It leads to incremental improvements to help lengthen the present customer experience life cycle, sometimes big changes and new customer experiences leadership strategies.

Developing Strategies and Tactics for Customer Interconnection

A customer-centered approach to creating positive interactions

"Be dramatically willing to focus on the customer at all costs, even at the cost of obsoleting your own stuff."

—Scott Cook, co-founder of Intuit

CHAPTER 6 Overview

Workday, USAA Insurance, Starbucks, Amazon, Netflix and ServiceNow have something in common	CX leaders' overarching customer experience strategies	Starting from your beginning	Customer-centered interconnection strategy and tactic development process	Develop strategies and tactics that cultivate customer interconnection

W orkday, USAA, Starbucks, Amazon, Netflix and ServiceNow have something in common: all have developed customer intelligence-driven strategies and tactics that create meaningful and valuable customer interconnections. Those interconnections then create high rates of growth, customer advocacy and profitability.

CX strategies are fundamental to driving revenue and the future of the organization and must be integrated with other core strategies such as marketing, sales, operations, finance, information technology, data management and business transformation. CX strategies are developed with customer engagement as a central input and the goal of customer interconnection should be supported by tactics at all interaction levels.

Successful interconnections between customers and businesses are positive, ongoing, reciprocal and meaningful to everyone involved. Customer experience makers are repeat innovators of interactions that create advocacy and deliver pleasing encounters that people want to have again and again. They do it with their leadership, culture and customer experience intelligence.

Many of the processes and actions used by customer experience leaders have become best practices. These best practices range from the secret to the well-known yet it is estimated that fewer than 20% of all businesses—regardless of size, location and industry—even use the more popular ones, leaving 80% under threat of marginalization or elimination by their better-performing peers.

This chapter is about a selected group of best practices that, when combined, guide the development of customer experience strategies and tactics by building meaningful interconnections with all the components of the customer experience continuum: a company's messages, people, processes, technologies, products and services.

Before getting into the specifics of applying selected best practices to develop strategies and tactics for customer interconnection, it will be helpful to look at the approaches of a few customer experience leaders.

CX leaders' overarching customer experience strategies

The original customer experience strategy of Starbucks was for their stores to be people's "third place to be" between home and work. The company modified this long-used and successful strategy in the time of COVID-19 by adding new "pickup" stores and expanding access to curbside pickup, drive-thru and walk-up counters. Then-Starbucks COO Roz Brewer explained this fundamental change: "Our relationship with our customers starts the moment they think of Starbucks." After this, the company wants to give safe, viable interaction options.

Brewer stressed the importance of the relationship between timely customer experience intelligence (CXI) and adaptive CX strategies and tactics: "We fully expect to learn as we go and further refine our plans in relation to specific locations, setup and the interplay of these different formats based on how customers continue to evolve their behavior." Then-CFO Pat Grismer added that, "We feel very good about the extraordinary data analytics our team has developed to allow us to rapidly learn and adjust as we go."[96]

Since its inception in the early 1990s, Amazon has been true to its fundamental customer experience strategy, ingraining it into its culture and priorities. As my co-author and I wrote in our book "The Customer Experience Revolution," Amazon has used three key strategies to achieve their lofty status. First, they were willing to sacrifice short-term gains to build long-term value. Second, they used data to drive the customer experience. Third, the company continues to innovate with new ideas to move closer to being the place to buy everything—books, electronics, music, clothing, household products ... everything.[97]

Workday, providers of advanced collaborative finance, HR and planning systems for businesses, describe their customer experience strategy as, "Once a customer is in production, we do everything we can to help them use, enjoy and value Workday. From education, training and enablement options to our collaborative Workday Community portal and support model, each aspect of the customer experience is designed to foster a relationship that lasts."[98] These are strategic summaries, not taglines, reflecting Workday's culture, commitment and priorities, and the company has the customer advocates, growth and profitability to show for it.

| Start from your beginning | → | Meaningful advice and training | → | Learn from across industries | → |

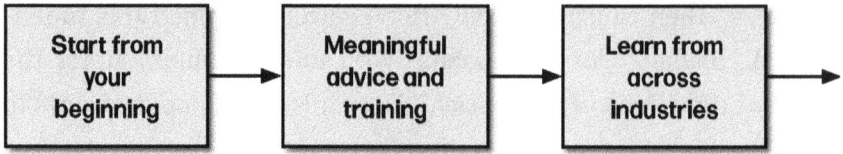

FIGURE 6.1 Determine and strengthen where your starting point is.

Starting from your beginning

So, how do you start your journey to identify, define and refine your organization's own set of customer experience best practices? Start from your beginning. To get the most from each stage of the process, carefully and objectively consider your starting point. It may be one from this list.

1) A new customer experience. Use the parts of the customer experience continuum—the interactions people have with your firm's messages, people, processes, technologies, products and services—to build a prototype of the experience you have in mind and then test it with customers.

2) Improve or innovate your current customer experience. You have decided that instead of competing on just price, product features, marketing campaigns or customer service, you want to protect your business and profit margins by improving or innovating the experience customers now have with your company. This is one of the most frequent starting points of commitment to customer experience transformation. At this stage, you may not have specific customers in mind. Many CX leaders have innovated based on their own disappointing personal experiences as customers or users of another company's products or services.

3) CX as a product life cycle extension. Perhaps you have a legacy product and would like to improve the interactions people have with it and other aspects of your business related to it.

This includes how people buy your product, how it is ordered, delivered and, if necessary, returned.

4) Surround your excellent customer service with excellent customer experience. If customers are already having pleasing interactions with your customer service people, expand this success to other interactions to bring them up to the same high standard so you can deliver a more positive end-to-end experience.

5) Your customer experience needs a refresh. Has your customer experience life cycle changed or shortened? Your personas may have evolved or some other variable has shifted—the economy, technology, fashion or the demands of your new customers. Or your competitors have caught up to or surpassed your once well-differentiated customer experience. Whatever the reason, you need to make your customer experience more relevant and valuable again.

6) You need to prove the concept of the customer experience effect. You've been the internal champion for customer experience and now you've selected a part of the business to make it happen and demonstrate that customer experience can work for your company and customers.

7) You are updating your business or marketing plan and want to add customer experience. This is a good time to consider some or all of the best practices of customer experience and the customer-centered process below to enhance what you already have.

8) Include customer experience as part of your start-up business. You have a business idea but you haven't formalized plans. This is an excellent time to consider the development of customer experience strategies and tactics to enhance how you will be differentiated and valued.

Meaningful advice and training

Another important early-stage effort is determining how much you and your organization know about the latest generation of customer experience. Adopt a definition of customer experience like the one offered in this book or create your own and share it with the people in your business.

After you have a formal and well-articulated description of your starting point but before you begin developing strategies and tactics with the customer-centered interconnection process, consider getting advice or training for every person important to your customer experience success. The training should be provided by qualified practitioners with a demonstrated knowledge of proven and successful customer experience including:

- customer experience intelligence development
- customer persona type creation and application
- baselining existing experiences and mapping competitors and prototypes
- measuring customer experience
- developing, testing and delivering out-of-box experiences
- customer experience innovation
- culture, leadership and decision-making at successful customer experience companies
- contextual change management based on your business starting point and what is learned during the advice or CX training sessions

The most effective results come when enough time is allowed for real-time reflection and discussion on advice or training in the context of the business. This is the opposite of quick-and-deep immersion. Taking the time up front will help internalize the concepts and increase engagement and the quality of outcomes.

Learn from other industries

Keep in mind that while many customer experience leaders are large and famous, they likely did not begin that way. Almost all were once start-up companies like Amazon, REI, Netflix and Workday.

Some well-established companies made a transformation later in their life cycle to have customer experience be their priority. Ally Financial started out in 1919 as General Motors Acceptance Corporation (GMAC), providing financing for automotive dealers. In the 1920s as the automobile market grew the company became involved in lending money to people who wanted to purchase automobiles. This was at a time when banks were not in the automotive loan business.

During World War II, the company switched who it served, adding railroads as financing customers. In the 1950s the company began loaning to consumers who needed to buy home appliances. Later in the 1950s, GMAC added auto loans. In the 1960s and '70s, it was financing vehicle protection and warranties. In the next 20 years, the company added mortgages. Their purchase of the Bank of New York led to the creation of their corporate finance division.

In the very early 2000s, GMAC's transformation took an enormous leap. In particular, the downturn in 2008 led to the company's separation from General Motors. And in 2010 the company was rebranded as Ally Financial and Ally Automotive. The transformation was not just about separation. It was about creating online and mobile experiences that business-to-business and consumer customers want to have. The company transformed into a top-rated online financial company.

There are many best practices and leadership attributes to learn from no matter where you are starting. And most customer experience best practices are applicable across industries.

Develop strategies and tactics that cultivate customer-business interconnection

Actively involving existing and future customers is at the center of developing effective strategies and tactics for customer interconnection. This customer-centered approach contributes insights and aids improvement and innovation decisions at the macro level as well as interaction-specific customer experience tactics. These inputs are critical to determine, develop and deliver extraordinary customer experiences. More specifically, the customer-centered interconnection process helps shape each piece of the customer experience continuum for different customer types or personas.

Companies innovate on a continuum that goes from intuitive to scientific. Their location on that continuum depends on corporate culture and the experiences of leadership. (For more about this see Chapter 7.) Most employ a hybrid model. It can start with an intuitive idea and put scientific rigor behind it or start with scientific rigor and then intuitively managing and improving. This combination and flexibility is a competitive advantage in developing and delivering desirable and profitable products, services and customer experiences.

Customer experience intelligence, both the intuitive and scientific kinds, is critical for creating effective CX strategies and tactics. As discussed in more depth in Chapter 3, insights from customer experience intelligence, including insights from thick-data methods, are used to create especially deep and wide customer information profiles also known as personas. Each profile represents many customers of a specific type. One persona could represent 20 people or millions with similar characteristics. Insights from CXI are used to guide strategy and tactical development along the important customer-centered interconnection process.

This process borrows from human-centered design, which is employed by many user experience (UX) experts to create, refine and assure effective and pleasing user interactions with machines, web-sites, enterprise software, automobile controls, mobile applications and more. The iterations of this process center around researching, designing and testing with people like the customers and users you want.

Many successful customer experience businesses also seek the input of people they describe as trusted individuals for their candor and insights. The iteration example of the process described below is one of several that, when completed, have developed strategies and tactics for each of the components that make up the customer experience. This includes the messages, people, processes and technologies, products and services that people interact with. This is done for specific customer types or personas.

> **Iterations are meant to move along
> quickly, not to be a long study.**

Iterations are meant to move along quickly. While "quickly" can vary between businesses, in any case an iteration is not meant to be a long study. It is at its best when the method and the people involved allow for several relatively fast rounds of research, development and testing. After each round, the goal is to quickly derive insights and make changes before moving on to the next iteration.

The customer-centered interconnection process differs slightly in scope and starting points from the research, design and test sequence used in human-centered design.

All three stages should be implemented with a combination of thick data and non-thick data inputs as discussed in Chapter 3. Include the customer experience four (CX4) as a minimum for desirable insight goals for each interaction type including use of the customer's time, range of emotions, do-for/do-to and value of the interaction.

Make empathy and the context of human interconnection a priority for more effective long-term outcomes. Design and consulting firm IDEO has advanced the ideas and practices of human-centered design (including creating the first mouse for Apple), placing empathy for the end-user of the resulting products at the center of their process. For IDEO, the key to figuring out what humans really want lies in doing two things:

1) Understanding people by observing them. For example, if you're designing a vacuum cleaner, watch people vacuum.

2) Putting yourself in the end-user's situation to understand what their experience is really like and feel what they feel.[99]

In the customer-centered interconnection process, these insights are used not just for products but for all customer interactions, digital and physical.

Adobe's Nick Babich puts the importance of customer-centered interconnection for software development this way: "When we design a new product, it's always essential to understand who and how people will use it. Without this understanding, there is almost no chance of creating a product people will love. 'People ignore design that ignores people' is a famous quote by Frank Chimero. And this quote perfectly summarizes the importance of user-centered design. User-centered design is about gaining a deep understanding of who will be using the product."[100]

Expanding Chimero's point, people will ignore customer experience that ignores people. More costly yet, people may use social media to warn other people to ignore the customer experience that ignores people.

When moving forward with developing customer experience strategies and tactics with the customer-centered interconnection process, be sure to apply one of the most effective attributes of design thinking, summed up by Jeanne Liedtka in a Harvard Business

Review article: "Identify hidden needs by having the innovator live the customer's experience."[101] When you select customer experience intelligence research methods, make sure they provide direct insights of human interaction and the related context.

> *"Identify hidden needs by having the*
> *innovator live the customer's experience."*

— **Jeanne Liedtka, faculty member at the University of Virginia's Darden School of Business and former chief learning officer at United Technologies Corporation**

Customer-centered interconnection strategy and tactic development process

Customer-centered interconnection strategy and tactic development is based on applying customer experience intelligence and selected best practices of human-centered development and innovation to determine, develop and deliver each of the components of the customer experience continuum for specific types of customers, users, patients or guests.

Overview

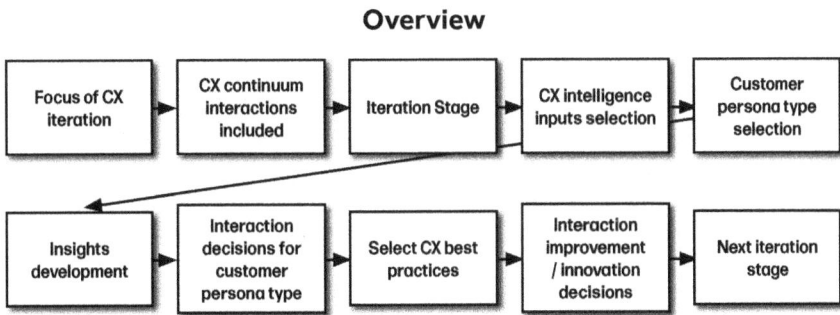

FIGURE 6.2 Overview of the customer-centered interconnection strategy and tactics development process.

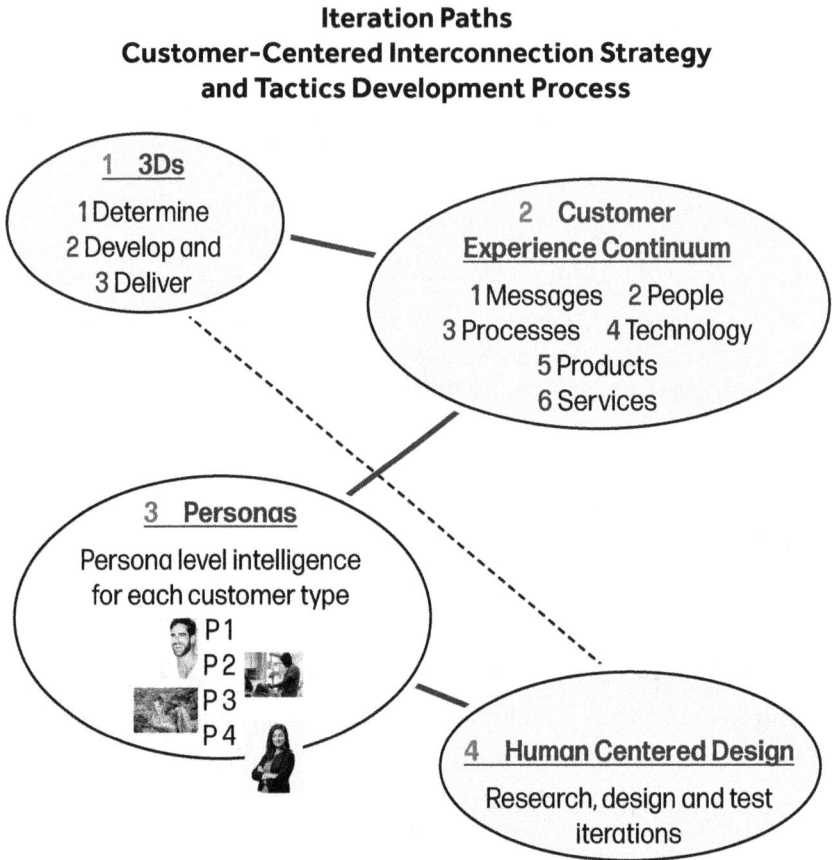

Iteration Paths
Customer-Centered Interconnection Strategy
and Tactics Development Process

FIGURE 6.3 The iteration paths of the customer-centered interconnection strategy and tactics development process used to develop customer experience strategies and tactics to determine, develop and deliver customer experiences for many companies and as part of the Customer Experience Course at the University of California at San Diego. The best practices of human-focused research, design and testing (in the development of software, websites, mobile apps and products) that user experience professionals use are now being applied by marketers and customer experience experts to develop all parts of the customer experience continuum.

Customer-centered interconnection strategy
and tactic development is based on applying
customer experience intelligence and selected best
practices of human-centered design to determine,
develop and deliver each part of the experience
for customers, users, patients or guests.

Customer Experience Strategy and Tactics Development Template Tool

Interaction name		Discovery	>	>	>	>	>	>	>
Interaction number	>	1	2	3	4	5	6	7
Off Internet	Interaction type							
	Interaction description							
On internet	Interaction type							
	Interaction description							
CX4 Leading interaction indicators and qualitatice and quantitative goals								
1 Value to Customer								
2 Emotional Goals								
3 Use of Customer Time								
4 Do For								
5 Likelihood to advocate								

FIGURE 6.4 Partial view of the customer or patient experience interaction evaluation template tool, the same as shown in Chapter 3. In its empty state, it gives a mental model and data-capture template of one of the many ways to illustrate the results from the process as you build a prototype of new interactions or change existing ones. Notably, buyer interactions can be non-linear and the same is true for the crossover between and simultaneous use of offline and online interactions. If this is found to be the norm for customer interactions, be sure your mental model and data-capture template reflect this.

The customer experience four (CX4), as described in Chapter 3, are the minimal set of criteria for each interaction. For health care applications, the patient experience five (PX5), adding physical criteria to the CX4, is the minimal set of categories for each interaction to be included.

The outcome goals to fix, improve or innovate existing customer interactions or determine new interactions are in large part based on the results of customer inputs (numbers and words) about the CX4 (or PX5) and additional selected information inputs from the customer-centered interconnection strategy and tactics development process. Or, with the results from the process, the customer experience strategy can be determined. Then the types of customer interactions and their goals are specifically defined to support the strategy. Certainly, the strategy and tactics can't be set without a realistic check for operational viability.

Likelihood to advocate—satisfaction goal is replaced with customer advocacy

An important part of using and implementing this customer-centered interconnection strategy and tactics process is to create advocacy from each interaction you develop. Customer experience leaders typically bypass customer satisfaction as a goal and replace it with customer advocacy. They keep in mind the say-do difference: that customer satisfaction is what customers will say or give a rating about; it is not a reliable predictor of advocacy. Advocacy is an active behavior. It's what customers will do to recommend your business to other people and have them become customers. It is a key part of the CX effect.

Even a high satisfaction score does not necessarily indicate a great customer experience. Satisfaction is simply the difference between what a customer expects and what they get. If expectations are low, then satisfaction can be high, even when the customer experience is poor. Don't measure your customer experience by your satisfaction rates. Instead, look at whether you are making your customers advocates. Advocates not only buy every product or service you offer that they can use, they also actively encourage others to do the same. The goal is to create advocates for your business by delivering a great customer experience.[102]

Gary Tucker, former SVP at consumer insights and data and analytics company J.D. Power and CEO at DealerRater, says, "Exceptional customer experience can best be measured by behaviors like active advocacy and loyalty. It is measured by what customers 'say and do.' Delighting customers across the entire experience can create active promotion, not only in the traditional social settings, but especially online ... through social media and third-party reviews."[103] Tucker stresses that merely satisfying a customer may prevent them from sharing your brand in a negative context or even earn you a casual endorsement, "delighting them across the entire experience can create active promotion, not only in the traditional social settings but especially online."

Don DiCostanzo, the innovative founder and CEO of Pedego, a leading manufacturer and marketer of electric bicycles, stresses the importance of aiming for customer advocacy in place of customer satisfaction: "Our vision is different from anyone else in this business," he says. "We want to make sure we delight our customers. We don't satisfy them but we delight them. That's a much higher bar. You must make sure that no one disappoints in the pipeline."[104] While this example is consumer-focused, the same is true for business-to-business companies and organizations needing to please patients and guests.

When working with businesses and their customers' experiences, and having interviewed people at many leading customer experience companies as educators and book authors, customer satisfaction has rarely come up as a solution for customer experience improvement and innovation. But customers purchasing again and actively advocating is an integral part of the strategic and tactical objectives and measures for CX excellence. It is not surprising that a top-performing CX firm can marginalize a competing organization that has high satisfaction ratings and low advocacy.

A loss hurts more than an equivalent gain

Richard Thaler, the Nobel Prize-winning behavioral economist, shares the following insights based on Daniel Kahneman and Amos Tversky's groundbreaking works on the relationship of human behavior and economics: "The fact that a loss hurts more than an equivalent gain gives pleasure is called loss aversion. It has become the single most powerful tool in the behavioral economist arsenal."

What is that ratio? Thaler's in-depth findings of how people do mental accounting reveals that "Losses hurt about twice as much as gains make us feel good."[105, 106] In order to create active advocacy, customer experience interactions need to make the customer feel good at a 3-to-1 ratio or more. The authors' CX research and work with many companies suggests that people need to be inspired to advocate 10 times by 10 interactions and then reminded or incented for the actual customer advocacy to occur once.

Percent of an Interaction Resulting in Customer Advocacy

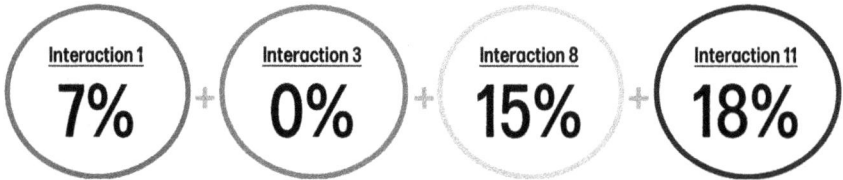

Interaction 1		Interaction 3		Interaction 8		Interaction 11
7%	+	**0%**	+	**15%**	+	**18%**

FIGURE 6.5 Percent of an interaction resulting in customer advocacy. If each interaction is developed to create a high likelihood of customer advocacy, it can add up to significant advocacy, growth, a lowering of marketing and sales costs and an increase in profitability.

> Thaler's in-depth findings of how people do mental accounting reveals that "Losses hurt about twice as much as gains make us feel good."[105, 106] In order to create active advocacy, customer experience interactions, on Internet and off, need to make the customer feel good at a 3-to-1 ratio or more.

Developing Strategies and Tactics for Customer Interconnection

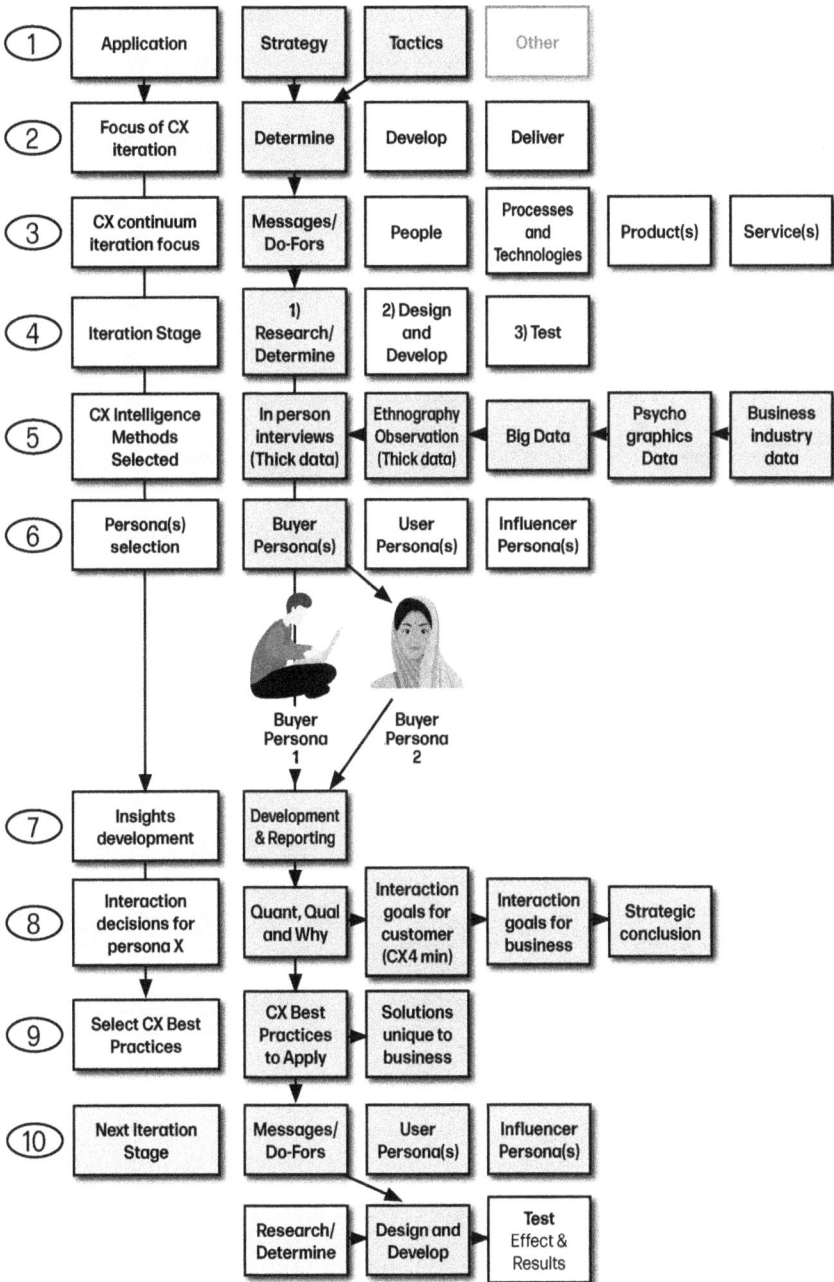

FIGURE 6.6 Developing strategies and tactics for the customer interconnection process.

The light blue or shaded boxes indicate the choices made at each stage of this customer-centered interconnection process iteration example.

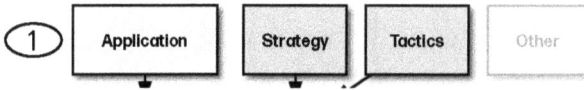

FIGURE 6.7 Application focus of the process.

Application of this process

In this example, select and focus on the purpose for which you will be using the process. Is it to develop your organization's customer experience strategy, tactics or both?

Another way to apply the process is to understand competitors' customer experience strategies, tactics, strengths and weaknesses. A sort of X-ray to identify opportunities. Customer experience leaders evaluate their existing competitors or potential competitors in other markets to find growth areas, such as Apple going into the smartphone business or Amazon's entry into grocery stores with Amazon Go and Whole Foods.

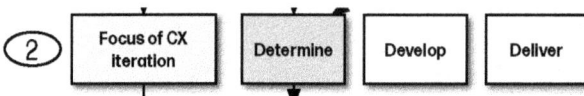

FIGURE 6.8 Focus of this iteration of the process is to determine the experience.

Focus the iteration process

Next is to focus the iteration process for customer experience creation. The choices are to determine the customer experience, develop it or deliver it. For this example, the process will be used to help determine what the customer experience should be. It's vital to have this intersection between the company and customer to determine what the customer experience should be. In the following process, you'll make decisions about the types of customers to determine the experience.

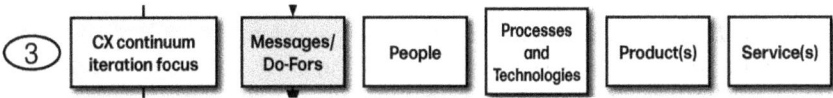

FIGURE 6.9 This example will focus on determining the messaging experience part of the customer experience continuum.

Customer continuum part(s) to be included

Next, consider the parts of the customer experience continuum to include in this iteration. The continuum includes the messages the company will use to engage and create customers. It also includes the employees that potential and existing customers will interact with, followed by the company's processes and technologies—their interactions with which are of paramount importance. The continuum is completed with the products and services people are offered. What these products and services promise to do is a key reason why people will decide to have an experience with your business and what they actually do for them is a key determiner of whether they will advocate for it.

This first round of iterations focuses on messaging, specifically, understanding what people value most about the customer experience and your products and services and what they do for them. Will the do-fors increase the chances that people are willing to pay for what is promised? And what would inspire customers to advocate for the company when having this interaction? The amount of time, resources and CXI businesses have may determine whether one, many or all the parts in the continuum will be included in the process going forward.

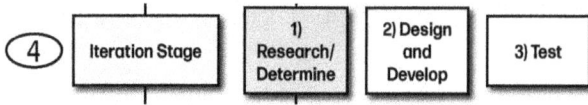

FIGURE 6.10 Step 4 concentrates on getting enough customer experience intelligence to create viable messaging in the next iteration, Design and Develop. The last iteration is testing the new design or prototype of the message.

Iteration stage

An iteration is a procedure in which repetition of a sequence of operations yields results successively closer to the desired result. In the context of customer-centered interconnection processes, the repetitions of a sequence of operations are not the same, by design. However, there are situations, like scaling or experimentation, where Iteration 1 will be purposely repeated exactly or with selected variables before moving on to Iteration 2. The same applies before moving on to Iteration 3.

Select the purpose of the iteration stage of the customer-centered interconnection process: 1) research/determine; 2) design and develop; or 3) testing. These stages are built on modified versions of the iteration stages used in human-centered design. They are in order and need to be completed individually for the best results. For this example, the process focus is on researching and determining what the messages should be.

At best, an iteration is quick, insightful and effective. The definition of quick is left to you and your organization and the condition of the related businesses and market opportunity windows. In any case, an iteration is not meant to be a long-term study. Too much time between iterations degrades the quality of the results. Interestingly, a by-product of an iteration can be the discovery of a new type of customer experience intelligence to include on an ongoing basis.

Iteration Paths
Customer Centered Interconnection Strategy
and Tactics Development Process

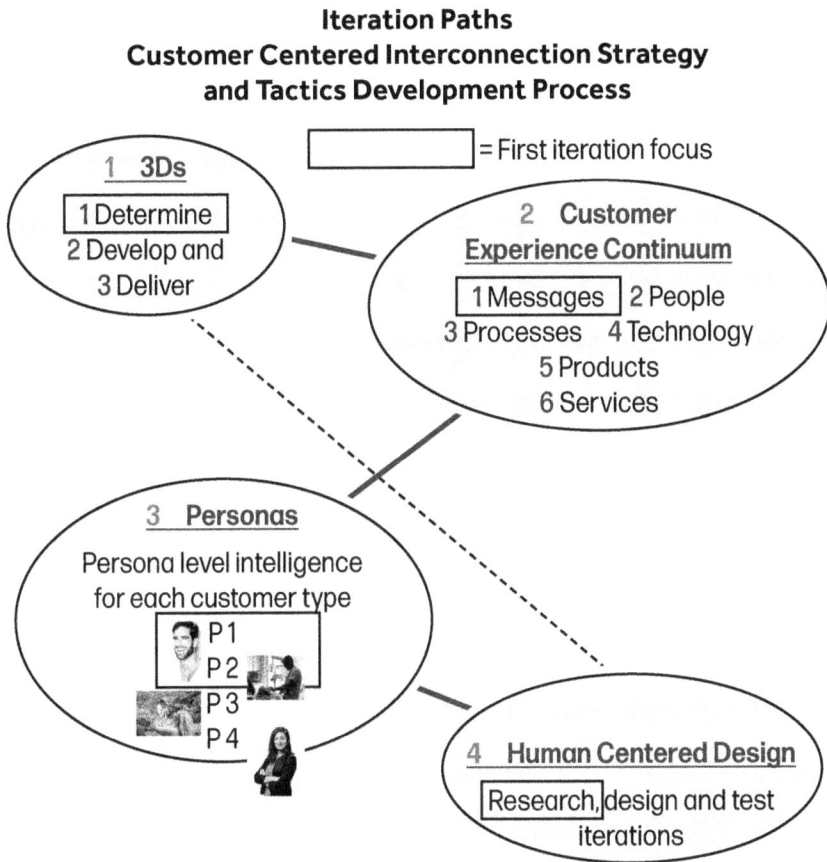

FIGURE 6.11 The iteration paths of the customer-centered interconnection strategy and tactics development process. The same as Figure 6.3, now with the boxed areas highlighting the interaction path and purpose of this iteration: To determine the messaging experience for Personas 1 and 2 with the selected inputs from and about these customers as research to develop the messaging.

Research/determine. This first stage of iteration, as highlighted in this example (Circle 4, #1) with rectangles, is research in search of a starting point for customer experience strategy and tactics. If you already have an idea or other starting point, then apply CXI to validate the idea in this stage. The goal is learning about insights that will help you determine what the interaction experiences should be along the continuum (Circle 2).

> **The first iteration will be to *determine* what the experience should be to please the customer.**
>
> **The part of the customer experience continuum what will be focused on will be the *messaging*.**

Design and develop. The second stage of iteration (Circle 4, #2) is dedicated to designing (developing) the customer experience continuum part(s) as determined in the first iteration. What is being developed? You can use terms like prototype, mock-up, first version, model, archetype or rough draft for what is being developed. Whichever term you select, be sure that what is being created is truly early-stage development. The goal is to gain insights at the outset so that you develop the interaction experiences with unbiased human input to not only create a pleasing experience but inspire customer advocacy.

This is the stage where the insights gained help guide a positive interconnection when customers interact with your prototypes. This is rapid prototyping—making minimum-viable prototypes of messages and interactions with your people, processes and technologies, products or services to be tested in the next stage (with specific customer types—personas).

Test. At this stage (Circle 4, #3) you apply the insights from the prior two stages and the prototypes from the development stage to test the relevant part or parts of the customer experience. It is important to have the qualitative and quantitative goals for each interaction for each customer persona type fully articulated at this point so they can be tested.

Be sure to include qualitative and quantitative goals for each interaction that customers care about. (See Chapters 3 and 6 for more on this.)

The testing will include the selected focus of this iteration. That may be communication messages, potential or existing customer interactions with your employees, processes and technologies. The focus of the testing is not only for functionality but for the all-important user experience. There are numerous established ways of testing products and services under development. Focus on achieving the all-important customer-centered interconnection.

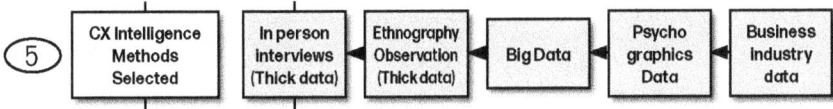

FIGURE 6.12 The CX intelligence methods selected. For more about this see Chapter 3.

Customer experience intelligence methods to be included in this process example

Which combination of CXI methods will you use to get insights from potential and existing customers? In this example, in-person interviews and ethnography (observation) are included to gather thick data that will provide information about people and capture quantitative, qualitative and human contextual information for successful interaction development and interconnection. These two methods complement the three other sources of selected data: big data, psychographic/lifestyle information and business industry data. The selection, recency and quality of the CXI methods are especially important. As is the way their input is transitioned to insights for decision-making.

FIGURE 6.13 The customer focus for this example is two buyer personas. The results will help decide more valuable ways they are different or alike for determining a pleasing experience for each.

Personas selection or creation

At this point, the focus will be on two customer experience buyer personas. In this example, the buyer personas are also the users of the product so there is no reason to have separate personas. The important influencer personas will be added in another iteration.

Buyer Persona 1 is a tech-savvy young man. Buyer Persona 2 is a well-educated young female who is extremely comfortable with different types of technology devices and software. For this example, the company has already started to create these personas. The insights gained in this process will help the business add information to each persona with the goal of gaining wide and deep knowledge for each customer type.

To summarize the selections in the customer-centered interconnection process so far:

1) The process will be used to assist in the creation of a customer experience strategy and tactics.

2) The focus of the first iteration is to help determine the customer experience (from the options of determine, develop and deliver).

3) The iteration stage focuses on determining what the messages and message experiences should be.

4) The development iteration stage uses research to determine the specifics of the messaging so it can be developed in the next iteration.

5) For this example, the CXI method used will be in-person interviews, ethnography/observations for the thick-data customer-centered view, along with big data, psychographic (lifestyle) data and business industry data.

6) There are many types of personas but for this example the focus will be on two types of buyer personas.

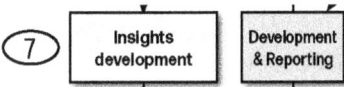

FIGURE 6.14 After the information from the customer experience intelligence methods has been completed (it may be part of ongoing CXI too!) it's vital that the findings be analyzed and then insights be developed and reported. With a degree of automation, the more accurate and quicker, the better, without losing context of the human experience.

Insights development for deciding strategy and tactics

The next stage is developing insights from the qualitative and quantitative data that has been created using the customer experience intelligence methods focusing on the two selected buyer personas. Use the interviews, ethnography, big data, psychographic information and business industry data to identify and articulate insights to help make effective decisions. In our example, the insights will be about determining messaging and related strategies and tactics to optimize the customer experience and reach business objectives.

Insights are created specifically for decision-making about the customer experience at two levels. One is the overall customer experience level and the second is about the specific messaging and the way people want to interact with it since this iteration stage is focused on researching/determining the messaging.

If this process is being used to baseline an existing customer experience, insights will be created for decision-making about the overall customer experience and for recommendations about specific interactions, such as leave it as-is, fix, improve or innovate.

The minimum granularity for developing or evaluating customer interactions is called the customer experience four or CX4. The CX4 include how the interaction(s) impact(s) the customer emotionally, in the value of having the interaction, what it does for or what it does to the customer and how it uses the customer's time (e.g., not well or very well). For a business in health care, the minimum granularity for developing or evaluating patient interactions is called the patient experience five or PX5. The PX5 add the fifth criteria to the CX4 of physical (e.g., pain to comfort; not cured or cured).

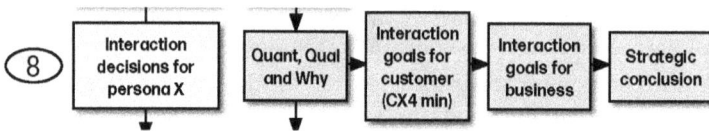

FIGURE 6.15 Decisions are made about the strategy, tactics, and customer interconnection with insights.

Developing overall customer experience strategy and interaction tactics

In this stage of the human-centered interconnection process insights are used to make decisions about the overall customer experience strategy and more specifically what this iteration stage of the process is focused on—researching/determining the messaging.

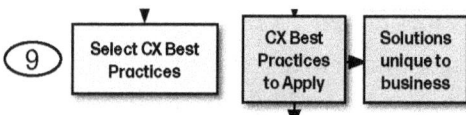

FIGURE 6.16 Explore customer experience best practices options to include for strategy, tactics and customer interconnection. Perhaps you have created some proven CX best practices too!

Select best practices and integrate them with solutions unique to the business

Now that the strategy has been developed based on customer experience intelligence and related insights, it is time to select the best practices of customer experience related to tactical messaging and messaging interactions.

Best practices exist because they are highly effective in getting superior results. If you are committed to transitioning to customer experience leadership, one of the most important and effective things you can do is to select best practices from the most successful customer experience companies and integrate them into your organization. There are hundreds of customer experience best practices. Establish quality sources of understanding and updating them.

Don't get distracted or discount the value of a best practice because it comes from a business in another industry or a company that serves a different market. Applying best practices from a cross-industry is a best practice itself.

Examples of customer experience best practices include:

- knowing your customers' expectations of customer experience;
- determining the customer experience before developing and delivering it (also known as the 3Ds);
- defining the unique concierge version of customer service for your customers;
- taking the jargon out of your internal language to get closer to customers;
- aligning your organization to provide extraordinary customer experiences;
- putting the customer and the experience at the center of evaluating the cost of every new initiative;
- having a clear definition of customer experience and be sure everyone in the company understands it; and
- blending the internet and off-internet experience.

This is a small sample of the universe of best customer experience practices to choose from and combine with your organization's solutions that are tailored to the business, product or service. For more about this see chapter 5: Best Practices in Customer Experience Leadership.

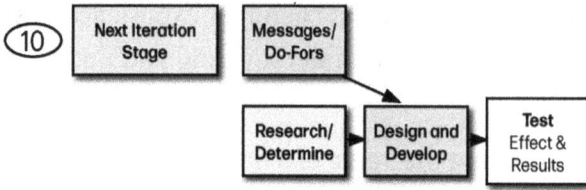

FIGURE 6.17 The next iteration stage is to develop the messages and messaging experience to be tested.

Preparing for the next iteration stage—designing and developing prototypes to be tested

After completing the first iteration, use the learnings to design and develop messaging. In this second iteration, it is extremely important to have real people representing their personas to help in creating the prototypes for the messaging that will be tested in the third iteration.

> The future of the process, and the present for some
> CX focused leaders, is that of being an integral
> part of how the company works in real-time.

Make it part of how you work and make decisions

Utilizing the results from the customer-centered interconnection strategy and tactics development process is transformative itself. The future of the process, and the present for a few businesses, is that of being an integral part of how the company works as a real-time contributor to customer experience decision-making and business results.

7

Innovating Customer Experiences

Ask, Watch and Listen, then anticipate and innovate

"We shared that same vision, the same values of hard work. To make it beautifully simple for the customer and for the user even if the user was totally unsophisticated."

—Scott Cook, co-founder of Intuit, describing one of the strong common values he shares with Intuit co-founder Tom Proulx

CHAPTER 7 Overview

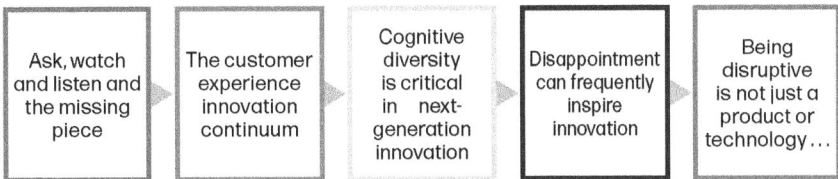

Ask, watch and listen and the missing piece	The customer experience innovation continuum	Cognitive diversity is critical in next-generation innovation	Disappointment can frequently inspire innovation	Being disruptive is not just a product or technology...

I f you want to do something and do it well, you need a clear definition of what you're trying to do. Ask 10 people to define customer experience innovation and you may well get 10 different answers. While some will be spot-on, others will be vague or ambiguous. But having a clear definition is required to successfully innovate customer experience.

Here is a look at some of the attributes that leading customer experience innovators have in common. These attributes, combined with best practices (Chapter 5) are helpful in forming your own definition in pursuit of customer experience innovation.

Some people believe their ideas are innovations; others declare that their inventions—the things they discover, find or build—are innovations. From a customer experience perspective, innovations are new interactions for people with parts of the customer experience continuum (messages; people; processes; and technologies, products or services) or the entire customer experience. These new interactions are adapted by customers in sufficient numbers to create significant market share, profitability and customer advocacy. In turn, the customer has benefitted in a way that they might have never thought about.

"The world's most innovative companies prosper by capitalizing on the divergent associations of their founders, executives and employees," as stated by Dyer, Gregersen and Christensen in their book "The Innovator's DNA."[107]

Add to this the impact of customer experience innovation as it changes people's lives for the better and inspires them to advocate for the company. Few people paying for and experiencing this type of innovation would give up being customers, even if the innovation was imperfect or they had some complaints about it. If successful, the new interactions are adopted by customers and, collectively as a market, they displace what was being done before. They redefine how the interactions will be done until another innovation displaces it. The new interactions have then made the transformation from invention to innovation.

The transformation from idea to invention to innovation

Defining Innovation from a business and customer experience perspective

Ideas ⇨ Invention ⇨ Innovation

FIGURE 7.1 Ideas to invention to innovation continuum.

True innovation in this context changes industries forever and, in more and more cases, creates new industries, new markets. In turn new customer and user expectations are created.

The companies and people involved in customer experience innovation not only have inspired energized customer advocates to work for them with word of mouth and social media but they also develop significant market share and, in the long run, profitability. Successful CX innovators marginalize or eliminate competition. This is how customer experience creates winners and losers in existing markets.

Examples of winners include Intuit, best known for their TurboTax and Quicken financial management products and services. Intuit seems to encompass many startups—a distinguishing and positive characteristic of this long-established company.

Look at Intuit's SnapTax. A small team at Intuit understood that there were many people, usually under age 35, whose tax returns required only simple, one-page forms. A significant number of them were also smartphone users. The company speculated and then confirmed that many potential customers would be open to the idea of uploading smartphone photos of their completed single-page tax returns to Intuit.

In turn, Intuit would convert this .jpg photo into data to populate the Internal Revenue Service (IRS) form and file it for the customer. This innovation was recognized by the IRS, which sent representatives to Intuit's San Diego offices to interview the people who innovated SnapTax.

At this point you might be thinking: With all its resources—including tax knowledge, a massive budget, vast amounts of data and a large workforce—why didn't the IRS innovate SnapTax? The short answer is that it comes down to priorities, leadership and culture. The IRS is a government organization focused on running its existing processes and getting tax revenues. For innovators, this means opportunity.

SnapTax turned out to be so successful that the company tested it with users of its TurboTax tax preparation software, many of whom typically have business tax returns of several pages. This too has been successful customer experience innovation.

Another example of CX innovation is Square. Square was founded by Twitter co-founder Jack Dorsey and Jim McKelvey in 2009 to serve micro-entrepreneurs and small businesses. The customer experience innovation idea was an easy method for using mobile devices for credit card payments. The result was an elegant and effective combination of off- and on-Internet customer interactions, from discovery (using promotions to help users discover the product through social media, word of mouth, etc.) to a simplified online application form for setting up a Square account, to receiving the small white card reader that plugs into a smartphone earbud jack. Prior to this, customers were stuck using clunky, expensive and overly complex point-of-sale solutions.

Square's engaging and fluid customer experience opened the market for mobile credit card readers to a variety of businesses. Square has a close relationship with another experience maker, Apple. Jack Dorsey and his team's approaches to innovating the mobile transaction customer experiences were part of the inspiration for Apple Pay. Now Square, another company blurring the lines between business-to-business and business-to-consumer companies, is a major player in the payments industry. In addition to its original card reader, Square has an iPad point-of-sale system and more advanced terminals that accept everything from chip cards to Apple Pay.

Square has a portfolio of merchant services including business debit cards, payroll software and loans through Square Capital.

Caviar, a Square brand, is a food delivery network and Square's consumer-facing mobile wallet, Cash App, has its own debit card.[108]

Ask, Watch and Listen and the missing piece

Along with Square, we have cited many other customer experience and user experience innovators in this book including SkimSure, Workday and ServiceNow. What do the people at these organization know and put into action about customer experience innovation that few others do?

When interviewing the customer behavior experts at independent research firm J.D. Power for the book "The Customer Experience Revolution," the company shared with us their new research report about customer intelligence called "Ask, Watch and Listen." Our enthusiasm for the concepts and methods behind Ask, Watch and Listen led us to seek permission from J.D. Power to use that title for our chapter on improving customer and user experiences. Ask, watch and listen to people is what most experience leaders did to fix and improve their customer and user experiences.

As time went by, it became apparent to us that something was missing in the ask, watch and listen concept. While it did indeed account for fixing and improving customer experiences, it did not explain how top-performing customer experience companies innovate.

Finding what was missing became a professional mission for us, one that entailed re-interviewing many of the people we consulted for "The Customer Experience Revolution" and the subsequent book "Customer Experience Rules!" We went through the interview transcripts, evaluated top-performing customer experience companies from the outside and several from within to locate the missing element. Using an aggregate view of the characteristics that leading customer experience innovators have in common, the missing piece turned out to be anticipation—ask, watch, listen ... and anticipate.

While there is not room in this chapter to include all of our findings, here are some of the most important qualities found in successful customer experience innovators and very likely next-generation CX innovators too.

Anticipate

Successful innovation goes beyond asking, watching and listening to current and would-be customers. Experience-maker companies do all those things. The successful innovators accurately anticipate what people want in their customer and user experience and how they want to be pleased by interactions with the company or organization, whether that's through its products or services, how it uses their time or makes them feel, and if they have a desire to have the interaction again.

The trouble is, people may not be able to tell you how or what to innovate for them. It is up to those creating the experience to anticipate what customers will like or will be pleasantly surprised by.

In working with successful customer experience companies and helping to transition other companies to a customer experience focus, we have found that the most effective leadership cultures include a high degree of cognitive diversity—that is, a mix of different viewpoints, skill sets, ways of thinking and approaches to problem-solving. This is combined with the ability to anticipate what customers would like in new interactions and what those interactions will do for them.

Intuitive through systematic—the customer experience innovation continuum

Our research has shown that the CX innovation takes place on a continuum. At one end is intuitive innovation. Intuitive innovation can happen at a planned time or an unplanned time (even the middle of the night, doing something completely unrelated) creating for the innovator what many call an "aha!" moment or apperception. While it is exciting to imagine that these instances happen on their own, they are generally inspired by vital inputs from the outside world.

**Customer Experience Innovation Continuum
Company Beginnings**

| Intuitive | Netflix
Uber
SkimSure
Square
Airbnb | Coursekey
Amazon
Intuit
Trader Joe's
Tesla | ServiceNow
USAA
Workday
Zappos
Ally Bank | Systematic |

FIGURE 7.2 Customer experience leaders positioned on the continuum based on how they were established.

At the other end of the continuum is systematic innovation. In systematic innovation there is a method or process, frequently a scientific one, that is purposely being used in an iterative way to innovate a new solution.

The people involved in this professional rigor usually have, in part or whole, responsibility for making discoveries. Most systematic innovation processes are based on the scientific method using controls and variables for discovery, testing and measuring outcomes. The rigor includes specific goals and time limits. The process frequently has budget limits too. It considers the timing of the demand in the market and customers' willingness to pay for what has been discovered, like technologies, customer experiences, products or services. All of this and more is included to determine the potential for return on investment and a go/no-go decision.

Most successful customer experience businesses fall in between the extremes of the continuum. They are hybrids—part intuitive and part systematic innovation.

Starbucks CEO and founder Howard Schultz intuitively innovated his idea for the company after a trip to Milan, Italy, in 1983. He witnessed the human networking that flourished at independent cafes, where people enjoyed drinking coffee and engaging socially and professionally in a comfortable setting. Since Starbucks' estab-lishment as a social networking coffee house in the United States in 1984, the company continuously innovates with a combination of intuitive and systematic techniques.

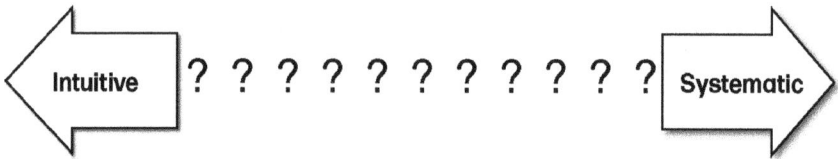

FIGURE 7.3 Where is your company on the customer experience innovation continuum? Is it where it needs to be?

Old-school or next-generation experience-maker innovation?

There are particularly important differences between most old-school or legacy company innovation and next-generation cus-tomer experience-maker innovation cultures.

Legacy companies typically assign specific people or teams to in-novate for the company. If an employee is not part of that team, they may not have a clear path for suggesting or getting support for new ideas. They may even risk being penalized for not doing their assigned job, as in "innovation is not in your job description; get back to work."

There is a transition from traditional to next-generation innova-tor. For "The Innovator's DNA," Dyer, Gregersen and Christensen[109] undertook a six-year study to uncover the origins of creative—and often disruptive—business strategies at innovative companies. They found "five discovery skills" that distinguish the most crea-tive executives: associating, questioning, observing, experimenting and networking. "We found that innovative entrepreneurs (who are also CEOs) spend 50% more time on these discovery activities than do CEOs with no track record for innovation. Together, these skills make up what we call the innovator's DNA. And the good news is, if you're not born with it, you can cultivate it."

There are two more important skills that can be added to Dyer, Gregersen and Christensen's five: anticipating and cognitive diversity. These seven skills help to describe the most effective customer experience innovators.

> **Origins of creative and often *disruptive business strategies***
>
> **Associating**
> **Questioning**
> **Observing**
> **Experimenting**
> **Networking**
> **Successfully anticipating and**
> **Cognitive diversity**

Aligned, all seven look like this: associating, questioning, observing, experimenting, networking, successfully anticipating and cognitive diversity.

> ***Old school legacy companies* assign people to innovate for the company. Some limit innovation to those people.**
>
> ***Next generation experience maker companies* assure that everyone can innovate on behalf of the customer, even if it is not their primary job.**

The achievements of next-generation experience-maker companies like Amazon, USAA, Square, Airbnb and Intuit are proof that everyone can innovate on behalf of the customer, even if it is not their primary job. In these businesses, culture and processes motivate people to contribute their ideas and viewpoints for customer experience innovation. Also, there is more freedom to fail and learn from failure.

In our work transitioning many client businesses to successful customer experience companies and interviewing numerous people from notable customer experience leaders for the books, it became apparent that there was another unique quality of most serial customer experience innovators: cognitive diversity.

Cognitive diversity

It was a service so advanced that it would change personal and business communications forever and crater our stock value. Early one morning a key competitor, who had been suspiciously quiet for a year, announced that a new all-in-one voice and data communications offering would be available to customers in six months. It was so futuristic that it was difficult even for our company's technology development experts to imagine.

We were a publicly traded Fortune 500 company and our ability to respond, or not, would put billions of dollars on the line, as well as customer confidence. Our leadership was nervous and wanted to respond in public as soon as possible.

In an hour our emergency response (ER) team was meeting to quickly discuss the situation and make a recommendation to company leaders. This special ER team consisted of eight experienced professionals representing diverse areas of expertise, skills and cultures. What's more, they were apolitical, focused on the question at hand and empowered by company leadership.

For our meeting each of us had reviewed the same dossier of information about our competitor's announcement and the same market and economic data and external information on customer demand. We went briskly around the table for individual takes on the situation and got, unsurprisingly, eight different views. In our typical quick and unbiased way of working together, we assembled our conclusion to report to leadership: because our competitor lacked the in-house technical expertise to make this all in one voice and data communications offer a reality, and our outside technology suppliers, the same as theirs, assured us that they would not have any of the enabling technology for several years, we concluded that our what our competitor announced was clever promotion of an offer that could not be available now or in the near future. A true paper tiger.

This announcement presented no immediate emergency but a short-term marketing challenge. Since our internal technology development expertise would make an all-in-one voice and data communications offer a reality in the next two to three years, this would give us an opportunity to be first in the market with this unique service. We would also have the advantage of pointing out to potential customers that we delivered on our promise of an available all-in-one voice and data communications offer while our competitor has yet to deliver on their aging promise.

This competitor had been struggling to innovate services customers wanted to pay for. Their stock price had languished and they were losing market share. The announcement, our team believed, was made to get attention and lift the stock valuation. We concluded it was a vision spun as an offer that would in six months disappoint customers and drag down our competitor's stock price. Don't overreact, we advised the leadership. We got creative and figured a way to benefit from the situation while reassuring our customers and prospects.

It was only a four-hour problem for us, thanks to our diverse team of experts and cultures, and I look back with pride on the work we did together in those surprise moments.

Cognitive diversity is critical in next-generation innovation

Cognitive diversity, as mentioned earlier, describes the differences in individuals' styles of processing and making sense of information.

Seven people may have seven perspectives based on the same incoming data and experiences, a situation not necessarily correlated to gender, ethnicity or age. Taking advantage of this range of viewpoints and ways of communicating enriches problem-solving by vastly expanding the range of possible solutions.

Author and effectiveness expert Sara Canaday summarizes her conclusions about cognitive diversity this way: "I've seen that companies produce the best results and are better able to innovate when their team members don't all think, process information or see the world in the same way. Leaders who innovate and make an impact seek out those who don't share their opinions and resist the tendency to over-rely on their experience and what has worked in the past."[110]

In their Harvard Business Review article, "Teams Solve Problems Faster When They're More Cognitively Diverse,"[111] Alison Reynolds and David Lewis affirm Canaday's views, saying that "a high degree of cognitive diversity could generate accelerated learning and performance in the face of new, uncertain and complex situations."[112]

It does. We have found this to be true with almost all leading customer experience companies and businesses newly focused on customer experience.

Still, cognitive diversity doesn't naturally occur in most organizations and companies often need to focus on identifying and overcoming barriers to it. Some of these barriers are purpose-built or systemic in the organizational structure, culture and values.

Reynolds and Lewis cite one all-too-common example of default bias restricting cognitive diversity: "We recruit in our own image. This bias doesn't end with demographic distinctions like race or gender or with the recruiting process, for that matter. Colleagues gravitate toward the people who think and express themselves in a similar way. As a result, organizations often end up with like-minded teams. When this happens ... we have what psychologists call functional bias—and low cognitive diversity."[113]

No matter their source, company leaders must dismantle the barriers to cognitive diversity and embrace it, tapping both intuitive and systematic ways of identifying cognitive differences and ingraining them into the culture and decision-making of the organization.

Aiming for employee advocacy

One of the most important factors in sustaining customer experience and innovation is your employee. If your customers, guests or patients have the same experience as your employees, how would that impact your reputation and bottom line? Some organizations are leaning toward next-generation employee experiences, including Airbnb, Salesforce and St. Jude Children's Research Hospital. [114]

A fast-growing number of software platforms are promising to help evaluate and improve employee experiences. While they can be very helpful, there first needs to be a genuine commitment to employee experience. As with customer experience, the company's leaders and culture must make desirable employee experiences a priority. The goal is not to merely satisfy and retain workers, it's to earn their advocacy during employment and after.

Based on direct observations and discussions with employees, customers and suppliers, we have found that high-performing organizations that excel in internal person-to-person, department-to-department service tend to also provide excellent external customer service experiences.

Customer and employee experience data research firm Qualtrics finds that, "Engaged employees understand what the customer wants too—in fact, research has shown that 70% of engaged employees indicate a good understanding of how to meet customer needs, compared to just 17% of disengaged employees."[115]

IBM's insightful report, "The Financial Impact of a Positive Employee Experience," finds that organizations that score in the top 25 percent on employee experience earn nearly three times the return on assets compared to organizations in the bottom quartile. The same top 25 percenters have double the return on sales compared to organizations in the bottom quartile. [116]

Next-generation employee experience change has been accelerated not only by employee demand but also by the growing development of indices that qualify and quantify employee experiences, helping employers define and better understand worker experiences and how they compare to the leaders and laggards.

The indices look carefully at many aspects of employee experience such as their sense of belonging and connection; meaning and purpose; impact on career; appreciation; sense of achievement; level of happiness; and energy. The outcomes of these measures can accelerate the improvement of employee experience and, in turn, customer experiences and innovation. Examples of employee experience index providers include Forrester[117], Future Forum[118], IBM[119] and Jacob Morgan[120]. Be sure to look carefully at the methodology of each one to understand how they are alike, how they are different and how they relate to you.

> **Serial innovators tend to lead with strategic investors over tactical expensers**

Serial innovators—are they strategic investors or tactical expensers?

Customer experience leaders who are serial innovators tend be companies that have a culture where the balance between people who are strategic investors and those who are tactical expensers is slightly tipped toward the former. Inside these companies is a positive edginess and excitement focused on what is next.

Strategic investors have a vision for the future and think strategically and imaginatively. Some say they see the big picture and the future. Others say they create it. Strategic investors look outside the company at what is going on in many areas such as technology, social trends, economics and much more. They do this naturally. They understand that investments need to be made and risks need to be taken to innovate. Strategic investors want to create the future now. They can, however, be somewhat detached from the practical and economic costs of doing this.

Tactical expensers look at costs. They usually have a set or sets of financial indicators they live by. They are risk-averse and do not like to upset the present financial indicators or other ratios, particularly when there is no positive short-term return on investment (in 90 days or the present year). Tactical expensers are most likely to want to save up for market share in a market created by another company. They tend to be internally focused on processes and programs and effectively practical.

Strategic investors and tactical expensers are two ends of an important spectrum impacting customer experience innovation. Combining the two in a more moderate position on that spectrum creates an openness to new ideas of customer experience strategies and interactions linked to business models and bottom lines in practical ways. This allows these companies to surpass others in which strategic investors and tactical expensers don't collaborate.

Disappointment can frequently inspire innovation
Disappointing customer experiences have motivated people toward successful intuitive and systematic customer experience innovation.

Pedego
In 2008, Don DiCostanzo founded the electric bike company Pedego, which has now passed annual revenues of $150 million with over 200 stores. In 2006, DiCostanzo was near age 50 and feeling

discouraged about riding his bicycle after staring at the large and long hills in his southern California neighborhood. Not wanting to be separated from his passion for riding, he purchased an electric bike (e-bike) in 2006 to help with the hills.[121] [15]

He thought the idea of an e-bike was excellent and exciting but he soon realized that his e-bike, like most of the others on the roads and trails, looked unappealing and was awkward to use. The e-bikes at that time were not designed for the people who were going to use them.

In 2007, DiCostanzo opened an e-bike store in Newport Beach, Calif., that became a kind of a learning lab for him. He confirmed that while people over 50 had enthusiasm and the resources for buying and using an e-bike, the present e-bikes weren't addressing everyone's needs. This, combined with the poor quality and ugliness of most e-bike models, inspired him to start Pedego.

"I was frustrated by the quality, and most importantly, the design of electric bikes that I came across in the market," he says. "I decided to set out on my own and start a company hyper-focused on producing and selling electric bikes, much like Tesla did when they decided to get into the business of only selling electric cars. I wanted to be the brand synonymous with e-bikes."[122]. And Pedego is that brand, with a very well-thought-out customer and user experience.

Square

Once again, a customer experience gone wrong inspired successful innovation. This time it was Twitter's Jack Dorsey, who had a friend who could not make a sale because he could not process an American Express card using the customer's smartphone. Based on that experience, in October 2010, Dorsey launched a system where anyone can accept credit card payment using a smartphone. Square mobile payments service was founded [123].

This wasn't just a system. Dorsey had specific financial and emotional goals for customers using Square, as he shared with Business Insider: "Payment is another form of communication. But it's never been treated as such. It's never been designed. It's never felt magical. About 90 percent of Americans carry cards, but almost nobody can accept them. We want to balance that out and just make payments feel amazing."

The overarching experience goal was to use technology to make life better based on humane and efficient customer interactions. Square processes over 2 billion card payments from 405 million payment cards annually for sellers. The company's point-of-sale ecosystem has more than 210 million buyer profiles and nearly 300 million items listed on Square by sellers. Square has reached a gross profit compounded annual growth rate of 49% over the past five years, had $103 billion in gross payment volume and more than 36 million monthly transacting active customers.[124]

CourseKey

Founded in 2014 by university students wanting to improve their own in-class experience and results, CourseKey solves many problems of today's classroom experience. Students collaborated with professors at San Diego State University to reinvent the college classroom and pedagogy in general. With a hope to no longer just "listen" to lectures, CourseKey lets both students and professors engage within the classroom through the hardware devices (a phone, tablet or laptop) they bring with them to class. CourseKey's technology applies behavioral analytics to improve student outcomes through location-based attendance, auto-graded assessments, interactive textbooks, social channels and analytics capabilities. This created an opportunity to change the way teachers and students participate in the classroom together. [125]

LPL Financial

In 1989, former Smith Barney broker Todd Robinson innovated the idea that financial advisors could be independent businesspeople. He created LPL Financial for entrepreneurial stockbrokers who wanted to break away from employment at companies like Merrill Lynch, Edward Jones, Morgan Stanley and Charles Schwab to build and run their own financial advisory businesses with their own base of clients.

LPL Financial provides independent financial advisors with the technology, research, service and support for their own businesses. LPL Financial does not have investment products of its own and is not affiliated with any bank.[126]

At the time, legacy companies scoffed at Robinson's idea but LPL Financial went on to attract a formidable number of financial advisors and their businesses in their early years. Viewing LPL's web site, the company is still true to what Robinson originally offered independent financial advisors. "We're building a future where advisors can, with no friction or complexity, as simple as turning the dials, pick the business model, services, technology and product mix that best meet their clients' needs."[127] Today LPL Financial represents major distribution accounts for companies offering financial products and services. It has over $1 trillion in brokerage and advisory client assets, serviced or custodied. And more than 19,000 financial professionals are serviced by the company.[128]

Uber

Travis Kalanick and Garrett Camp created the idea for Uber while having trouble hailing a car in Paris in 2008. What they wanted to do at that time was instantly be able to tap a button and have their ride come to them. Why not?

And that is what they did by creating a new personal transportation service with an exemplary combination of on- and off-Internet customer experience, flipping the dispatcher/customer model.

While the company has experienced growing pains there is no doubt they have gone beyond creating an app to request rides to changing the expectations of customer experience and logistics. The logistical idea is to use technology to give people what they want, when and where they want it.[129]

As of this writing, Uber is still on our "CX ones to watch" list for profitability. It is continuing to progress with significant improvements in adjusted earnings before interest, taxes, depreciation and amortization.[130] Uber has 93 million users who use the firm's ridesharing or food delivery services at least once a month. The company is also well-positioned to benefit more from its valuable user data, according to independent research and valuations firm Morningstar.[131]

Intuit

With one year left to go in college, and inspired by Steve Jobs, Stanford University engineering student Tom Proulx wanted to start a PC software company. "I was really excited about the prospect of something that would be a mass-market kind of product that millions of people would use," he says.[132]

Scott Cook, with a bachelor's degree in economics and mathematics from the University of Southern California and an MBA from Harvard Business School, had worked for Procter & Gamble. There he gained experience and insights about product development, market research and marketing. His next position was working at Bain & Company close to Stanford University. He had an idea for a software-based business. He was looking for programmers. He went to the Stanford engineering library looking for a place to put his posting for programmers wanted.

Proulx was sitting in front of the Stanford engineering library, working on a group project. That's where Proulx and Cook informally met. Cook asked Proulx where a good spot for the posting would be. Proulx was interested in the business idea related to the posting. Cook explained the genesis of it to Proulx, "My wife has the idea of writing a program to automate the routine day-to-day financial tasks that every household has to do. Paying bills, keeping a check register, tracking your spending. Just the basic stuff that we all have to do." It was instantly obvious to Proulx "that was the idea I was looking for!"[133]

The combination of Proulx and Cook meeting and Cook sharing his wife's idea was the intuitive founding and initial innovation for a financial software and services company most people now know for QuickBooks, TurboTax and SnapTax.

While Proulx and Cook share the same vision and values, they describe themselves as diagonally opposite, with complementary strengths and weaknesses. They focused on the idea that software should be so intuitively obvious that people just know how to use it without any instruction. In 1983, this was very different thinking. It was to be the beginning of a new era in the customer experience revolution.

SkimSafe and SkimSure
As we profiled in Chapter 1, Björn Granberg's frustration after his credit card information was stolen by data thieves led to the founding with partner Carl Martinsson of their business SkimSafe in Europe and SkimSure in the United States in 2016. The young company has generated more than $7 million since then.

Being disruptive is not just a product or technology, it's a profitable business model
It's been over 20 years since the well-accepted idea of being "disruptive" has been associated with innovation. The concept of disruptive innovation, published in the Harvard Business Review in 1995, was architected by Clayton Christensen with co-authors Michael Raynor and Rory McDonald.

Since that time, there have been many misapplications of the idea that innovating takes place by being disruptive—with a product, service, technology or some other way. We hear and see this all too frequently. Christensen, Raynor and McDonald clarify that being disruptive is a process that "originate(s) in low-end or new-market footholds."[134] Whether opening a market to underserved customers or creating new customers, just being disruptive is not the point. The innovation needs to have the capability to mature into profitability. It needs to deliver the product and services with customer experience that is up to or surpasses existing expectations and best practices.

A bit more insight from Christensen, Raynor and McDonald: "Disrupters tend to focus on getting the business model, rather than merely the product, just right. When they succeed, their movement from the fringe (the low end of the market or a new market) to the mainstream erodes first the incumbents' market share and then their profitability."[135]

> **Thinking about being disruptive as a complete business model, including customer and user experience increases the chances of real innovation success.**

Thinking about being disruptive as a complete business model, including customer and user experience and sustainable customer adoption and advocacy, increases the chances of real innovation success. Some well-thought-out disruptive business models take time to ramp up and have impact. This plays into the blind spot of legacy companies minding their present success and processes.

Some of these companies, internally focused and coasting on legacy product or service offerings, are taken by surprise as their shares of market, number of customers and profitability fall to experience makers. The old-guard companies, many of whom can bleed red ink for a long time, keep doing what has brought them success in the past. They are not able to understand that the currency of the market and its business model, unrecognized or seemingly odd to incumbents, has changed. Changed because a well-thought-out disrupter has raised the bar of customer expectations and has an effective business model too. "The fact that disruption can take time helps to explain why incumbents frequently overlook disrupters," according to Christensen, Raynor and McDonald.[136]

Create next-generation customer experience leadership now
While companies like ServiceNow, Pedego and USAA are innovating next-generation customer experiences today, the time for you to start down a path to joining them is now. Join them by leveraging a thorough understanding of next-generation customers with customer experience intelligence. Learn about behavioral economics and customer experience best practices and make them part of your insights and decision-making processes.

Next, move forward by developing strategies and tactics for positive customer interconnection and advocacy creation. This will help guide you in innovating customer and user experiences for next-generation customers. Make it your goal to be on the road to customer experience leadership!

> **Customer experience—the best practices, results and the profession—will keep evolving and reinventing new ways to understand customers and anticipate what innovations people will embrace in the future.**

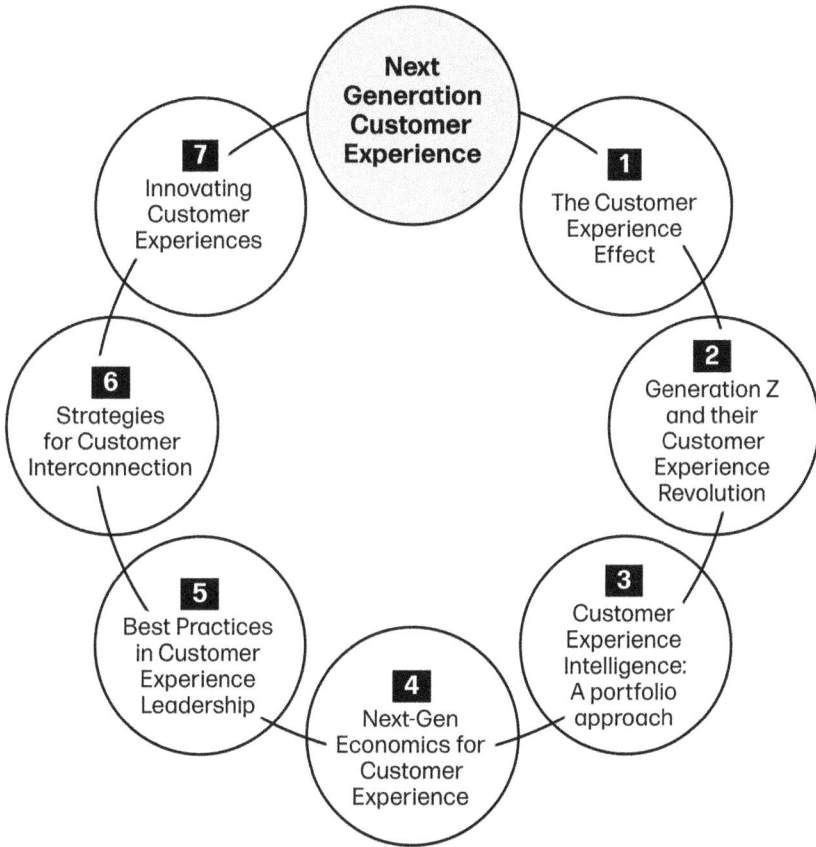

FIGURE 7.4 Essentials for sustainable next-generation customer experience leadership.

Customer experience—the best practices, results and the profession—will keep evolving and reinventing new ways to understand customers and anticipate what innovations they will embrace in the future.

As next generation customer experience moves forward, outstanding and sustainable results are likely to come from organizations committed to a hybrid of established best practices and new ways of determining, developing and delivering experiences to customers. And they will be doing it while aiming for customer experience leadership in turbulent times.

Customer Experience-First Markets

The number of markets where organizations can waffle on investing in customer experience will decline as Gen Zs become the dominant customers.

Customer experience-first markets—where leading companies have created demand for a pleasing customer experience above all else—yield winners and losers. Low prices and special offers are still important but are now secondary to people getting an extraordinary experience from interacting with the company. We have seen this in markets such as video rental, business and consumer tax services, smartphones, taxi services and mobile payments. The customer experience effect played an important role in changing expectations decisively. Gen Zs will significantly accelerate the number of customer experience-first markets. People and companies that commit to being next-generation experience makers will be on the right and profitable side of this change.

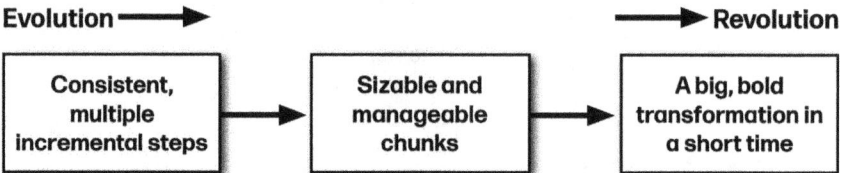

Evolution ⟶   **⟶ Revolution**

| Consistent, multiple incremental steps | → | Sizable and manageable chunks | → | A big, bold transformation in a short time |

FIGURE 7.5 CX focus and transformation continuum.

Companies must evolve. Deciding whether you choose evolution or revolution is up to you and how much time you have to pursue or create opportunities. From making customer experience a priority with consistent, multiple incremental steps or moving quicker with sizable and manageable parts of the organization or taking big, bold steps in a short time.

Customer experience is the new currency and companies can't compete without it. There will be a few that go beyond being financially successful to being significant to their customers' lives. They will purposely help define the next generation of customer experiences. Is it you? Is it your organization? We hope it is!

References

1. Spitznagel, E. (Jan 25, 2020). Generation Z is bigger than millennials — and they're out to change the world. NewYorkPost. https://nypost.com/2020/01/25/generation-z-is-bigger-than-millennials-and-theyre-out-to-change-the-world/
2. The Smithsonian Museum of Arts and Industries. Arts + Industries Building. Washington, D.C. (June 5, 2022) "Futures" Exhibit
3. Dolbee, S. (May 5, 2020) What makes a good leader? San Diego Tribune p.6 https://www.sandiegouniontribune.com/lifestyle/story/2020-05-10/sandi-dolbee-on-leadership
4. Picoult, J. (October 2021). 2021 Watermark Consulting Customer Experience ROI Study. Watermark Consulting, Retrieved January 24, 2022, https://watermarkconsult.net/wp-content/uploads/2021/10/Watermark-Consulting-2021-Customer-Experience-ROI-Study.pdf
5. Hayes, A. (February 22, 2021) Investopedia—Business, Marketing Essentials – Brand Equity definition. https://www.investopedia.com/terms/b/brandequity.asp
6. Interbrand. Best Global Brands 2020, [company brand valuation index and report]. https://learn.interbrand.com/hubfs/INTERBRAND/Interbrand_Best_Global_Brands%202020%20Desktop.pdf
7. Interbrand. Best Global Brands 2021, [company brand valuation index and report]. https://interbrand.com/best-brands/
8. PWC. (2017-2022) The Future of Customer Experience. https://www.pwc.com/future-of-cx
9. Schmidt-Subramanian, M. (January 28, 2021). Forrester Research: What's The ROI of CX Transformation? Forrester Blog. https://go.forrester.com/blogs/whats-the-roi-of-cx-transformation/
10. Deloitte. Monitor Deloitte (2018). The True Value of Customer Experiences, p. 2. https://www2.deloitte.com/content/dam/Deloitte/us/Documents/process-and-operations/us-cons-the-true-value-of-customer-experiences.pdf

11. Deloitte. (July 2017) Wealth Management Digitalization changes client advisory more than ever before. p-5. https://www2.deloitte.com/content/dam/Deloitte/de/Documents/WM%20Digitalisierung.pdf

12. Aten, J. (Aug 30, 2020) The 9 Simple Words That Made Amazon a Trillion-Dollar Company Amazon Prime started off with the simple idea that 'we hope to earn even more of your business.' It seems to have worked. Inc. https://www.inc.com/jason-aten/the-9-sinple-words-that-made-amazon-a-trillion-dollar-company.html

13. Bean, J; Van Tyne, S. (2012). The Customer Experience Revolution, How Companies Like Apple, Amazon, and Starbucks Have Changed Business Forever, Brigantine Media. p. 52-53

14. Macker, N. (Nov 2, 2020). Morningstar Stock Analysis Report, Analyst Note. p. 1

15. Microtrends. ServiceNow: Number of Employees 2010-2021. Retrieved July 26, 2021. https://www.macrotrends.net/stocks/charts/NOW/servicenow/number-of-employees

16. ServiceNow. (October 28, 2020) Press Release. Third Quarter 2020 Financial Results. Retrieved July 26, 2021. https://www.servicenow.com/company/media/press-room/servicenow-reports-third-quarter-2020-financial-results.html

17. Spitznagel, E. (Jan 25, 2020). Generation Z is bigger than millennials — and they're out to change the world. New York Post. https://nypost.com/2020/01/25/generation-z-is-bigger-than-millennials-and-theyre-out-to-change-the-world/

18. Catalyst. (March 2021). Generations: Demographic Trends in Population and Workforce https://www.catalyst.org/research/generations-demographic-trends-in-population-and-workforce/

19. Parker, K. and Igielnik, R. (May 14, 2020). On the Cusp of Adulthood and Facing an Uncertain Future: What We Know About Gen Z So Far. https://www.pewsocialtrends.org/essay/on-the-cusp-of-adulthood-and-facing-an-uncertain-future-what-we-know-about-gen-z-so-far/

20. Hanbury, M. (July 16, 2019). Gen Z is leading an evolution in shopping that could kill brands as we know them. https://www.businessinsider.com/gen-z-shopping-habits-kill-brands-2019-7

21. Viens, A. (Oct 2, 2019). Social Media by generation. https://www.weforum.org/agenda/2019/10/social-media-use-by-generation/

22. Kasasa. (July 6, 2021). Boomers, Gen X, Gen Y, Gen Z, and Gen A explained. https://www.kasasa.com/exchange/articles/generations/gen-x-gen-y-gen-z

23. Insider Intelligence. (April 4, 2022). US Gen Z social media user stats (2020 – 2025). https://www.insiderintelligence.com/charts/us-genz-social-media-users/

24. Reynolds, K. (November 1, 2021). Facebook wants to attract young people, but Gen Z teens say it's a 'boomer social network' made for 'old people'. https://www.insider.com/facebook-gen-z-teens-boomer-social-network-leaks-2021-10

25. Twenge, J. (2017). iGen Why Today's Super-Connected Kids Are Growing Up Less Rebellious, More Tolerant, Less Happy—and Completely Unprepared for Adulthood

26. American Psychological Association. (October 2020). Stress in America 2020. "Stress in America 2020 report"

27. Stone, M. (May 18, 2021). Gen-Z: They Crave Stability and Trust, So Give It To Them. https://www.forbes.com/sites/michaelstone/2021/05/18/gen-z-they-crave-stability-and-trust-so-give-it-to-them/?sh=721e7908594a

28. Reynolds, K. (November 1, 2021). Facebook wants to attract young people, but Gen Z teens say it's a 'boomer social network' made for 'old people'. https://www.insider.com/facebook-gen-z-teens-boomer-social-network-leaks-2021-10

29. Vocabulary. (2022). Vocabulary.com dictionary. https://www.vocabulary.com/dictionary/interaction

30. Bean, J. and Van Tyne, S. (2012). The Customer Experience Revolution, How Companies Like Apple, Amazon, and Starbucks Have Changed Business Forever. Brigantine Media. p. 14

31. McCarthy, E. (March 12, 2020). Alan Alda would like your attention—The 84-year-old actor has spent his career playing the smart guy. Now he wants to share some wisdom. The Washington Post. https://www.washingtonpost.com/lifestyle/2020/03/12/alan-alda-would-like-your-attention/

32. Wang, T. (Aug 2, 2017). The human insights missing from big data. YouTube. https://www.youtube.com/watch?v=pk35J2u8KqY

33. Foote, S. (June 20, 2005). Historian and Novelist, Dies at 88. The New York Times.

34. Foote, S. (February 13, 2003). A Writer's Life, C. Stuart Chapman, University Press of Mississippi, 1st Edition. Kindle. p. 2655

35. Norman, D. (April 21, 1994). Things That Make Us Smart: Defending Human Attributes in the Age of the Machine, Basic Books. Kindle. p. 3327

36. Norman, D. (April 21, 1994). Things That Make Us Smart: Defending Human Attributes in the Age of the Machine, Basic Books. Kindle. p. 3340

37. Gartner Glossary. (2021). Gartner.com dictionary. https://www.gartner.com/en/information-technology/glossary/artificial-intelligence

38. Mims, C. (July 31, 2021) https://www.wsj.com/articles/why-artificial-intelligence-isnt-intelligent-11627704050. p. B2

39. Interactions Corp. (February 23, 2020). Conversational AI. https://www.interactions.com/conversational-ai/

40. Gartner Glossary. (2020,2021). Gartner.com dictionary. https://www.gartner.com/en/information-technology/glossary/dark-data

41. Meehan, M. (June 4, 2019). What Your Data Isn't Telling You: Dark Data Presents Problems and Opportunities for Big Businesses. Forbes. https://www.forbes.com/sites/marymeehan/2019/06/04/what-your-data-isnt-telling-you-dark-data-presents-problems-and-opportunities-for-big-businesses/?sh=7138480e484e

42. SAS Analytics Solutions. (February 23, 2020). Natural Language Processing (NLP). https://www.sas.com/en_us/insights/analytics/what-is-natural-language-processing-nlp.html

43. IBM. (February 9, 2020). Analytics, Prescriptive analytics. https://www.ibm.com/analytics/prescriptive-analytics

44. Gualtieri, M. (February 2, 2017). What Exactly The Heck Are Prescriptive Analytics? Forrester. https://go.forrester.com/blogs/17-02-20-what_exactly_the_heck_are_prescriptive_analytics/

45. Aten, J. (January 19, 2021). This Is Steve Jobs's Most Controversial Legacy. It Is Also His Most Brilliant. When you should listen to your customers. https://www.inc.com/jason-aten/this-was-steve-jobs-most-controversial-legacy-it-was-also-his-most-brilliant.html

46. Bean, E. and Bean, J. (July 28, 2021). 19th Global Conference: Brussels. Leadership in Turbulent Times. International Leadership Association. https://ilaglobalnetwork.org/events/brussels/ p.74

47. Thaler, R. H. (Retrieved April 7, 2022) THE NOBEL PRIZE—Richard H. Thaler Biographical. https://www.nobelprize.org/prizes/economic-sciences/2017/thaler/biographical/

48. Pinto, B. (December 7, 2021) The Chicago School of Professional Psychology, Insight, 6 Career Paths with a Master's in Behavioral Economics, What is Behavioral Economics? https://www.thechicagoschool.edu/insight/career-development/6-career-paths-with-a-masters-in-behavioral-economics/

49. Gino, F (2017, October 10,) The Rise of Behavioral Economics and Its Influence on Organizations, Harvard Business Review. https://hbr.org/2017/10/the-rise-of-behavioral-economics-and-its-influence-on-organizations

50. Max Witynski, M. (Retrieved November 18, 2021) Behavioral economics, explained, University of Chicago News https://news.uchicago.edu/explainer/what-is-behavioral-economics

51. Max Witynski, M. (Retrieved November 18, 2021) Behavioral economics, explained. What are the origins of behavioral economics research, and who are Tversky and Kahneman? University of Chicago News. https://news.uchicago.edu/explainer/what-is-behavioral-economics

52. Max Witynski, M. (Retrieved November 18, 2021) Behavioral economics, explained. What are the origins of behavioral economics research, and who are Tversky and Kahneman? University of Chicago News. https://news.uchicago.edu/explainer/what-is-behavioral-economics

53. Thaler, R. H. (June 14, 2016) Misbehaving: The Making of Behavioral Economics W. W. Norton & Company, p4 Kindle Loc 147

54. Thaler, Richard H. (June 14, 2016) Misbehaving: The Making of Behavioral Economics W. W. Norton & Company, p6 Kindle Loc 172

55. Hansson, Prof. G. K., Secretary General of the Royal Swedish Academy of Sciences. (October 9, 2017). The Sveriges Riksbank Prize in Economic Sciences in Memory of Alfred Nobel 2017, Announcement of the 2017 Prize in Economic Sciences to Richard H. Thaler. https://www.nobelprize.org/prizes/economic-sciences/2017/prize-announcement/

56. Stitch Fix. Job posting. Lead UX Researcher. LinkedIn. (Retrieved February 7, 2022) https://www.linkedin.com/jobs/view/lead-ux-researcher-at-stitch-fix-2667687463/

57. Thaler, R. H. (June 14, 2016) Misbehaving: The Making of Behavioral Economics W. W. Norton & Company, p44 Kindle Loc 1274

58. Thaler, R. H. (June 14, 2016) Misbehaving: The Making of Behavioral Economics W. W. Norton & Company, p164 Kindle Loc 2647

59. Thaler, R. H. (June 14, 2016) Misbehaving: The Making of Behavioral Economics W. W. Norton & Company, p34 Kindle Loc 623 and p.50 Kindle Loc 1002

60. Walsh, J.W. & Keller-Birrer, V. (2006-2019; Retrieved November 18, 2021) Behavioral Economics in the Digital World. International Institute for Management Development. p1 https://www.imd.org/contentassets/01dd818a256e428ca7c853e11055812f/tc038-19-print.pdf

61. Steve Jobs at the 1997 Apple Worldwide Developers Conference (WWDC). Steve Jobs Customer Experience. YouTube video upload Oct 16, 2015. https://www.youtube.com/watch?v=r2O5qKZlI50

62. Third-wave economics: The real-time revolution (October 23, 2021) The Economist. p21 https://www.economist.com/briefing/2021/10/23/enter-third-wave-economics

63. Third-wave economics: The real-time revolution (October 23, 2021) The Economist. p22 https://www.economist.com/briefing/2021/10/23/enter-third-wave-economics

64. Third-wave economics: The real-time revolution (October 23, 2021) The Economist. p21 https://www.economist.com/briefing/2021/10/23/enter-third-wave-economics

65. Third-wave economics: The real-time revolution (October 23, 2021) The Economist. p21 https://www.economist.com/briefing/2021/10/23/enter-third-wave-economics

66. Texas Rangers Guest Guide. (Retrieved October 21. 2021). Guest Guide Welcome. https://www.mlb.com/rangers/ballpark/guide

67. Arizona Diamondbacks Baseball Team. FromThisSeat.com (Retrieved Oct 18, 2021) Breakdown of the Chase Field Seating Chart. https://www.fromthisseat.com/index.php/blog/19902-breakdown-of-the-chase-field-seating-chart

68. Bean, J; Van Tyne, S. (2012). The Customer Experience Revolution, How Companies Like Apple, Amazon, and Starbucks Have Changed Business Forever, Brigantine Media. p.109

69. Schultz, H. and Gordon, J. (March 29, 2011). Onward: How Starbucks Fought for Its Life Without Losing Its Soul. Rodale Inc.

70. Bean, E. and Bean, J. (October 13, 2017). 19th Global Conference: Brussels. Leadership in Turbulent Times. International Leadership Association (ILA). https://ilaglobalnetwork.org/events/brussels/ p.74

71. Best Upon Request. Retrieved June 15, 2022. Employee Concierge Services. https://www.bestuponrequest.com/employee-concierge/

72. Gartner (2022). Gartner.com dictionary. http://www.gartner.com/it-glossary/big-data/

73. The World's 50 Most Innovative Companies 2014. Retrieved June 15, 2022. https://www.fastcompany.com/most-innovative-companies/2014/sectors/big-data

74. The Firms' Most Wanted: Big-Data Scientist. (Aug 9-10, 2014). Wall Street Journal. p1

75. Schumpeter. (July 19, 2014). Little things mean a lot: Businesses should aim for lots of small wins from "big data," that add up to something big. The Economist. p.60

76. Aton, J. (August 30, 2020). The 9 Simple Words That Made Amazon a Trillion-Dollar Company. Amazon Prime started off with the simple idea that 'we hope to earn even more of your business.' It seems to have worked. Inc. magazine. https://www.inc.com/jason-aten/the-9-sinple-words-that-made-amazon-a-trillion-dollar-company.html

77. Kang, C. (February 28, 2022). Here comes the full Amazonification of Whole Foods. The New York Times. https://www.nytimes.com/2022/02/28/technology/whole-foods-amazon-automation.html

78. Keyes, D. (October 2, 2019). Amazon is looking to install its Go technology in hundreds of retail stores by 2021. Business Insider. https://www.businessinsider.com/amazon-looking-to-license-go-technology-to-retailers-2019-10?op=1

79. BBC. (February 20, 2020). Larry Tesler: Computer scientist behind cut, copy and paste dies aged 74. https://www.bbc.com/news/world-us-canada-51567695

80. Markoff, J. New York Times. (February 2, 2020). Lawrence Tesler, Who Made Personal Computing Easier, Dies at 74. https://www.nytimes.com/2020/02/20/technology/lawrence-tesler-dead.html

81. IDEO. (December 4, 2018). IDEO's human centered design process: How to make things people love, User Testing. https://www.usertesting.com/blog/how-ideo-uses-customer-insights-to-design-innovative-products-users-love

82. Bean, J; Van Tyne, S. (2012). The Customer Experience Revolution, How Companies Like Apple, Amazon, and Starbucks Have Changed Business Forever, Brigantine Media. p.116

83. Krug, S. (December 24, 2013). Don't Make Me Think, Revisited: A Common-Sense Approach to Web Usability (3rd Edition) (Voices That Matter)

84. Bean, J. (2015). Customer Experience Rules! 52 ways to create a great customer experience! Brigantine Media. p.37, 38

85. de la Mare, N. (2009) (retrieved July 30, 2021). What Lego Can Teach Us. AdAge. https://adage.com/article/on-design/lego-teach/138047

86. Interaction Awards. Interaction Design Association (IxDA) Archive (retrieved July 30, 2021). http://awards.ixda.org/past-years/

87. Gassam Asare, J. (December 7, 2018). Diversity, Equity & Inclusion,—Diversity, Equity & Inclusion. Forbes. https://www.forbes.com/sites/janicegassam/2018/12/07/the-best-places-to-work-for-2019/#8fc26fe528f9

88. Recruit Holdings HR Technology Division. (Retrieved July 30, 2021). Best Places to Work 2021, San Diego, Glassdoor https://www.glassdoor.com/Award/Best-Places-to-Work-San-Diego-LST_KQ0,19_IL.20,29_IM758.htm

89. Fortune 100 Best Companies to Work For 2019. Forbes. (Retrieved July 30, 2021). https://www.greatplacetowork.com/best-workplaces/100-best/2019

90. Fortune 100 Best Companies to Work Forbes 2019. USAA Profile [updated]. (Retrieved July 2021). https://www.greatplacetowork.com/certified-company/1100166

91. IBM Corporation. (2018). IBM Analytics Thought Leadership Whitepaper. IBM Smarter Workforce Institute. The Employee Experience Index—A new global measure of a human workplace and its impact. https://www.ibm.com/downloads/cas/QDAVJA5E

92. Morgan, J. (May 11, 2017) (Retrieved July 30, 2021). These Are The Top Companies For Employee Experience, 15 companies stand out from all others, here's who they are! https://www.inc.com/jacob-morgan/these-are-the-top-companies-for-employee-experience.html

93. Johnson, D. (February 27, 2019) (Retrieved July 30, 2021).The Employee Experience Index. Forrester. https://go.forrester.com/blogs/the-employee-experience-index/

94. IBM Corporation. (2018). IBM Analytics Thought Leadership Whitepaper. IBM Smarter Workforce Institute. The Employee Experience Index—A new global measure of a human workplace and its impact. p.4. https://www.ibm.com/downloads/cas/QDAVJA5E

95. The Customer Advisory Board. (Retrieved July 30,2021). What is a Customer Advisory Board? https://customeradvisoryboard.org/#1580820927787-67e114e3-feee

96. Kelso, A. (June 10, 2020). Starbucks Redefines Its 'Third Place' Strategy To Adapt To The Coronavirus Crisis. Forbes, https://www.forbes.com/sites/aliciakelso/2020/06/10/the-coronavirus-crisis-has-caused-starbucks-to-shift-its-real-estate-strategy/#4a11df50197c

97. Bean, J; Van Tyne, S. (2012). The Customer Experience Revolution, How Companies Like Apple, Amazon, and Starbucks Have Changed Business Forever, Brigantine Media. p. 109

98. Workday, Inc. (2020). How Workday Reimagined the Customer Ownership Experience, [downloadable PDF file]. p.6 https://www.workday.com/content/dam/web/en-us/documents/other/ebook-customer-ownership-experience.pdf

99. UserTesting. (December 4, 2018). IDEO's human centered design process: How to make things people love. https://www.usertesting.com/blog/how-ideo-uses-customer-insights-to-design-innovative-products-users-love

100. Babich, N. (Oct 18, 2019). User Centered Design Principles & Methods. Adobe. https://xd.adobe.com/ideas/principles/human-computer-interaction/user-centered-design/

101. Liedtka, J. (September–October 2018). Why Design Thinking Works—It addresses the biases and behaviors that hamper innovation. Harvard Business Review, https://hbr.org/2018/09/why-design-thinking-works

102. Bean, J. (2015). Customer Experience Rules! 52 ways to create a great customer experience! Brigantine Media. p.69

103. Bean, J. (2015). Customer Experience Rules! 52 ways to create a great customer experience! Brigantine Media. p.69-70

104. Hogan, D. (May 9, 2022) (Retrieved March 10, 2023). This E-Bike Life blog. Pedego Palooza Brings E-Bike Customers Together. https://thisebikelife.com/pedego-electric-bikes-palooza-event/

105. Thaler, R. H. (June 14, 2016) Misbehaving: The Making of Behavioral Economics W. W. Norton & Company, Chapter 4: p.34

106. Thaler, R. H. (June 14, 2016) Misbehaving: The Making of Behavioral Economics W. W. Norton & Company, Chapter 7: p.59

107. Dyer, J., Gregersen, H., Christensen, C. (December 2009). The Innovator's DNA. Harvard Business Review Magazine. https://hbr.org/2009/12/the-innovators-dna

108. Fast Company. (February 24, 2022). https://www.fastcompany.com/company/square

109. Dyer, J., Gregersen, H., Christensen, C. (December 2009). The Innovator's DNA. Harvard Business Review Magazine. https://hbr.org/2009/12/the-innovators-dna

110. Canaday, S. (June 18, 2017). Cognitive Diversity. What's often missing from conversations about diversity and inclusion.https://www.psychologytoday.com/blog/you-according-them/201706/cognitive-diversity

111. Reynolds, A and Lewis, D. (March 30, 2017). Teams Solve Problems Faster When They're More Cognitively Diverse. https://hbr.org/2017/03/teams-solve-problems-faster-when-theyre-more-cognitively-diverse

112. Reynolds, A and Lewis, D. (March 30, 2017). Teams Solve Problems Faster When They're More Cognitively Diverse. https://hbr.org/2017/03/teams-solve-problems-faster-when-theyre-more-cognitively-diverse

113. Reynolds, A and Lewis, D. (March 30, 2017). Teams Solve Problems Faster When They're More Cognitively Diverse. https://hbr.org/2017/03/teams-solve-problems-faster-when-theyre-more-cognitively-diverse

114. Morgan, J. (February 2, 2022). The Employee Experience Index. https://thefutureorganization.com/employee-experience-index/

115. Qualtrics. (June 2019). How to show the impact of your employee experience campaign on your customers.https://www.qualtrics.com/uk/experience-management/employee/engagement/impact-on-customers/

116. IBM Corporation and Globoforce Limited. (2018). The Financial Impact of a Positive Employee Experience. https://www.ibm.com/downloads/cas/XEY1K26O

117. Weader, J. (September 1, 2020). The Employee Experience Index. https://www.forrester.com/blogs/tag/employee-experience-index/

118. Elliott, B. (October 7, 2020). Findings from the Remote Employee Experience Index. https://futureforum.com/2020/10/07/rewiring-how-we-work-building-a-new-employee-experience-for-a-digital-first-world/

119. IBM Analytics. (July 2017). The Employee Experience Index. https://www.ibm.com/downloads/cas/JDMXPMBM

120. Morgan, J. (2022). The Employee Experience Index. https://thefutureorganization.com/employee-experience-index/

121. Pedego Press Release (February 1, 2022) (Retrieved March 13, 2023) Pedego CEO Don DiCostanzo Selected as Entrepreneur of the Year from Ernst & Young. https://pedegoelectricbikes.com/press/pedego-ceo-don-dicostanzo-selected-as-entrepreneur-of-the-year-from-ernst-young/

122. Reiss, R. (Apr 23, 2021) (Retrieved March 10, 2023) Pedego CEO On Reinventing The Wheel. Forbes Leadership Strategy, Forbes Magazine. https://www.forbes.com/sites/robertreiss/2021/04/23/pedego-ceo-on-reinventing-the-wheel/?sh=7fc363f6118a

123. Dickey, M. (Oct 3, 2012). (Retrieved February 28, 2022). Meet Jack Dorsey, The Visionary Behind Twitter and Square. Business Insider. http://www.businessinsider.com/how-jack-dorsey-came-to-invent-square-and-twitter-2012-9

124. Square. (June 15, 2021). Notice of Annual Meeting of Stockholders, p.31

125. Craft Data. (Retrieved February 28, 2022). CourseKey [profile and data]. https://craft.co/course-key

126. Bean, J; Van Tyne, S. (2012). The Customer Experience Revolution, How Companies Like Apple, Amazon, and Starbucks Have Changed Business Forever, Brigantine Media. p. 102, 103

127. LPL Financial. (Retrieved February 28, 2022). LPL Financial home page. https://www.lpl.com/

128. LPL Financial. (Retrieved February 28, 2022). About LPL Financial. https://www.lpl.com/about-Us.html

129. Uber. (Retrieved February 28, 2022). Uber About Us. https://www.uber.com/our-story/

130. Feuer, W. (March 8, 2022). Uber Raises Its Guidance Citing Covid Bounce Back. The Wall Street Journal. pB3

131. Mogharabi, A. (February 11, 2022). (Retrieved March 7, 2022). Uber Morningstar Analyst Note—Uber's Moat Sources Not Running Out of Fuel. https://www.morningstar.com/stocks/xnys/uber/quote

132. YouTube. DraperTV. (June 13, 2015). (Transcript accessed March 1, 2022). The Origin of Intuit, Intuit Founders Scott Cook & Tom Proulx. https://www.youtube.com/watch?v=JB8t133I1TI

133. YouTube. DraperTV. (June 13, 2015). (Transcript accessed March 1, 2022). The Origin of Intuit, Intuit Founders Scott Cook & Tom Proulx. https://www.youtube.com/watch?v=JB8t133I1TI

134. Christensen, C.M., Raynor, M., & McDonald, R. (December 2015). What Is Disruptive Innovation? Harvard Business Review [Reprint R1512B], p.5

135. Christensen, C.M., Raynor, M., & McDonald, R. (December 2015). What Is Disruptive Innovation? Harvard Business Review [Reprint R1512B], p.6

136. Christensen, C.M., Raynor, M., & McDonald, R. (December 2015). What Is Disruptive Innovation? Harvard Business Review [Reprint R1512B], p.6.

Acknowledgments

To the University of California San Diego Division of Extended Studies:

A special thank-you to the people at the University of California San Diego, Division of Extended Studies, for the tremendous support for the idea and development in 2015 of one of the first university-quality courses in customer experience leadership for domestic and international students. The course has focused on the best practices of leading customer experience companies, independent research and outside-the-class effectiveness. This includes over 180 customer experience evaluation and recommendation projects. Projects for early-stage and established businesses (consumers and business clients), healthcare and public organizations in more than 15 countries.

To my wife Joanne. For your encouragement and enormous contributions that have made this book possible.

A very special thank you to Vineetha Raveendran for her unwavering partnership throughout this project, from research/analysis of Generation Z customers and experiences. And for authoring the chapter about Generation Z and their customer experience revolution.

To all the Generation Z enthusiasts for the great discussions about their customer experience journey and for helping us understand how different they are from the previous generations.

Paige Boyd—mom, educator, customer service and customer experience insights. For your high energy, focus and commitment to quality interviews.

Thaís Imagawa, marketing manager, Wireless Services, São Paulo, Brazil. For your amazing passion for customer experience, quality research and critical input throughout.

Cathy Zumberge, human resources educator and consultant. Your support, questions and input has been invaluable.

Michael Thompson, M.D., orthopedic surgery, Scripps Health, hand surgeon extraordinaire.

David A. Bean, editorial consultant, for your creative and analytical input always with specific readers in mind.

Wendy Eichenbaum, senior manager experience design, TA Digital Transformation Consultancy; and principal user experience (UX) strategist and designer, Ucentric Design, San Diego, Calif. For your input and insights about user experience, customer experience and behavioral economics.

The following people made invaluable direct contributions to this book with their support, input, sharing experiences or expertise:

- Samir Asaf, Ph.D., CFA, managing director, Del Morgan; adjunct professor of finance, Stanford Continuing Studies
- Federico Cesconi, founder and CEO, SANDSIV customer intelligence solutions
- Joely Gardner, Ph.D., CEO and chief user researcher of Human Factors Research
- Björn Granberg, co-founder and co-CEO, SkimSafe (Europe) and SkimSure (USA)
- Tina Goldstone, director of marketing, Interbrand
- Daniel Binns, CEO NA and global director of partnerships at Interbrand

- Liraz Margalit, Ph.D., social psychologist, behavioral design, and decision-making
- Joseph Rydholm, editor, Quirk's Media
- Teena Singh, senior manager of customer insights and adoption, ServiceNow

Index

The letter "f" in a page number refers to a figure as in 33f2.1

Additional customer experience leadership books by and with Jeofrey Bean

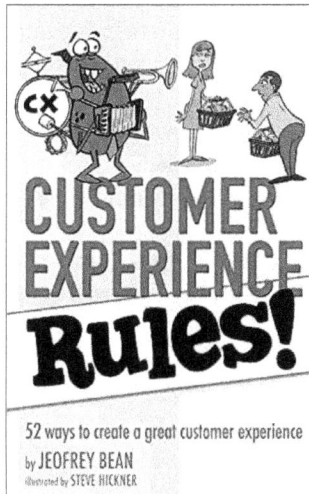

In "Customer Experience Rules!," CX expert Jeofrey Bean gives 52 best practices for a company to create a great customer experience. Going beyond branding, customer service and customer satisfaction, the customer experience encompasses every touchpoint a customer has with a company. Follow these rules in your business to craft the very best customer experience possible. Bean shares innovative yet practical insights about effective customer experience strategy and tactics from the leaders to improve customer engagement, loyalty and advocacy: including Uber, Tesla, Amazon, Qualcomm, Kaiser Permanente, DealerRater, Imprivata, Ford, Starwood

Hotels and more. Like his best-selling CX book "The Customer Experience Revolution," "Customer Experience Rules!" is based on the author's experience, research and in-person interviews with companies recognized for CX innovation. Read one rule a week—or all 52 at once! "Customer Experience Rules!" is your guide to customer experience success. Bean is the author of two customer experience books that help companies whether they are beginning to learn about CX or are well on the way to integrating customer experience into the DNA of the company.

PRAISE FOR "CUSTOMER EXPERIENCE RULES!"

"Whether you are new or a long-time practitioner of customer experience, this book is a great introduction and reminder of all the best practices we should use—every day!"

— Dann Allen, Vice President, Customer Experience, Bank of the West

"'Customer Experience Rules!' is a must-have book for companies beginning to focus or companies refocusing on the experience of the customer."

— Deborah Schoonover, Customer Success Manager, Freund Container & Supply

"If you worship at the altar of customer experience, these are your 52 weekly devotionals."

— Rob Scruggs, former Director, Customer Experience, E*Trade Financial

"One of the best Customer Service books of all time"

—BookAuthority, 2019

"One of the best Customer Experience books of all time"

—BookAuthority, 2019

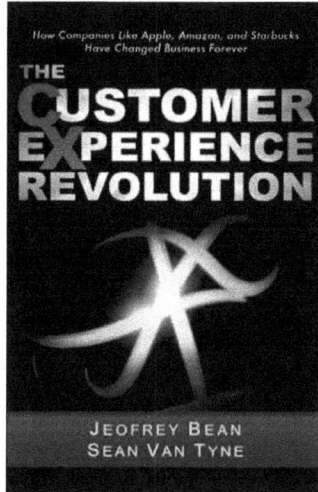

How Companies Like Apple, Amazon, and Starbucks
Have Changed Business Forever

THE

**CUSTOMER
EXPERIENCE
REVOLUTION**

JEOFREY BEAN
SEAN VAN TYNE

The customer experience revolution has begun! Businesses that provide an extraordinary customer experience are more profitable and sustainable than their competition. They dominate industries and marginalize competing companies. In their innovative book "The Customer Experience Revolution: How Companies like Apple, Amazon and Starbucks Have Changed Business Forever," authors Jeofrey Bean and Sean Van Tyne uncover valuable insights about leadership and decision-making. At large and small companies they call Experience Makers, the focus has surpassed products, services and price toward the purpose-built customer experience and the user experience within it. Customer experience is an all-encompassing term that goes beyond traditional definitions of marketing, customer service, customer satisfaction and product development.

Delivering extraordinary customer experience is becoming more and more important, according to J.D. Power and Associates. We know from the data that people will pay for it, says Gary Tucker. Unique to customer experience books, Bean and Van Tyne capture the key elements of customer experience through interviews with business leaders.

The book shows how Starbucks CEO Howard Schultz spearheaded a customer experience strategy using social media that built tremendous customer loyalty. An interview with executive Larry Tesler reveals the leadership qualities of Steve Jobs at Apple and Jeff Bezos at Amazon. It shows how Reed Hastings at Netflix brought down Blockbuster and continues to stay competitive. The book tells the story of Square (founded by Jack Dorsey of Twitter), as well as many other companies, including Intuit, LPL Financial, Skinit, EMN8, IDriveSafely and more.

These profiles of leaders in companies both large and small show the value of creating a complete customer experience ecosystem. Bean and Van Tyne found 12 essential leadership qualities common to the best companies in total customer experience management. They insist that these best practices can no longer be ignored for a company to remain successful. Customer expectations have risen and will continue to change. "The Customer Experience Revolution" shows why every business needs to make customer experience an integral part of its business strategy.

PRAISE FOR "THE CUSTOMER EXPERIENCE REVOLUTION"

"'The Customer Experience Revolution' is a book that everyone who wants to succeed in business must read."

— **Todd Robinson, Founder and Former Chairman, LPL Financial**

"Companies that delight their customers outperform their peers. This guidebook tells us why and how they do it in industries as diverse as retailing, smartphones, food service and driver education. I highly recommended it to anyone building a customer-focused business or refocusing an existing business on the experience of the customer."

— **Larry Tesler, Larry Tesler Consulting, former Vice President and Chief Scientist, Apple Computer**

"One of the best Customer Service books of all time"

— **BookAuthority, 2019**

About the Author

J eofrey Bean is an accomplished customer experience (CX) and marketing expert, advisor, and acclaimed book author of "Customer Experience Rules! 52 Ways to Create a Great Customer Experience;" "The Customer Experience Revolution: How Companies Like Apple, Amazon, and Starbucks Have Changed Business Forever," with Sean Van Tyne; and "Next Generation Customer Experience: How Companies Like ServiceNow, Netflix and Intuit are Creating Next-Generation CX Now," with Vineetha Raveendran.

He advises small innovative businesses through Fortune 500 corporations in making effective and profitable marketing and customer experience decisions with consulting, training, and seminars. Jeofrey is known for practical and innovative results that improve or transform marketing and interactions customers, patients, and guests have on the internet and off.

He is an internationally recognized instructor and mentor at the University of California San Diego Division of Extended Studies teaching Advanced Marketing and Customer Experience Leadership in domestic and international programs.

As an engaging and informative speaker, Jeofrey delivers thought leadership, insights, and commentary with a dash of humor. Venues include the International Leadership Association, JD Power Annual Service Awards Conference, LPL Financial Focus Conference, Scripps Health, Stanford University, Bloomberg Radio, National Public Radio, WNYC, and CX Punk Chat and Fireside Chats podcasts.

About Vineetha Raveendran

Vineetha Raveendran is known for her commitment to developing quality research-based insights leading to effective marketing, sales operations, and customer experience results in special collaborations and at companies in the technology industry.

With the research, analysis and the writing of the chapter "Generation Z and their Customer Experience Revolution," she is a major contributor to the customer experience leadership book "Next Generation Customer Experience: How Companies Like ServiceNow, Netflix and Intuit are Creating Next-Generation CX Now."

Vineetha is fluent in English, four Indian languages, and basic Spanish. She earned a master's degree in international business from the PSG College of Arts and Sciences and a Business Management Certificate from the University of California San Diego Division of Extended Studies.